Ten More Doors

For Elizabeth —
Keep knocking!

Deke
Feldman

Ten More Doors
Politics and the Path to Change
A Memoir

Copyright © 2021 Dede Feldman
All Rights Reserved

Published by:
Latilla Publishing
Albuquerque, NM

Trade Paperback
ISBN: 978-0-9995864-2-6

EBook ISBN: 978-0-9995864-3-3

Library of Congress
Control Number: 2021912878

220 pages, 30 images

Women in Politics • Progressive Campaigns • Southwest

Design: Charlie Kenesson

Photos and Illustrations:

Christina Weeks (author photo)

Cary Herz (page 11)

Charlie Kenesson (page 77)

Courtesy of Legislative Council Services (page 102)

Dean Hanson ©*Albuquerque Journal*,
reprinted by permission (page 103)

Cartoon by *Albuquerque Journal's* John Trever,
reprinted by permission of cartoonist (page 144)

Singli Agnew (page 153)

All other photos Dede and Mark Feldman

POLITICS
AND THE
PATH TO
CHANGE

A Memoir

Dede Feldman

From the Foreword to *Ten More Doors:*
Politics and the Path to Change

"It is my hope that this memoir will seal Dede's legacy
on the list of New Mexico progressive reformers and
spur a younger generation of activists to see the value in
perseverance and good, old-fashioned stubbornness—no
matter how many people say, "It can't be done!"

—Stephanie Garcia Richard,
New Mexico Commissioner of Public Lands

Praise for Inside the *New Mexico Senate:*
***Boots, Suits and Citizens* (2014)**

"...Dede Feldman has pushed hard and effectively as a
fighting reformer and former state senator in New Mexico—and now with this insightful peek into the inner
workings of that legislative chamber, she's encouraging
all of us to join the fight."

—Jim Hightower, populist speaker,
writer and editor of the *Hightower Lowdown*

"Completely honest and highly informative.
Dede Feldman is a first-rate observer and chronicler."

—Former US Senator Fred Harris

"A unique history of the New Mexico Senate...Senator
Feldman is a skilled and insightful writer."

—New Mexico Governor Michelle Lujan Grisham

Praise for *Another Way Forward:*
***Grassroots Solutions from New Mexico* (2017)**

"...former Senator Dede Feldman continues to shape our
political future by showing how people all across New
Mexico are creating solutions when those in power fail
to step up and do so. ...Anyone who is losing hope for
New Mexico—and the nation—should read this re-
minder that together, we can make a difference."

—Tim Keller, Mayor of Albuquerque

*For Abby, and all those fierce
millennials and members of Gen Z*

Foreword

I REMEMBER A PARTICULAR SUMMER DAY in Dede and Mark Feldman's Jemez mountain home, food overflowing their tiny kitchen, at least two dozen curious voters perched with paper plates on knees to hear from me—the newly minted Democratic legislative candidate for the surrounding district—as I tentatively began to tell them all how I was a force to be reckoned with. I told them how I would defeat the popular, ten-term Republican legislator who currently represented them. I told them how I would stand up for the forests and the canyons as well as the people. I lost that race but went on to win many more, finally achieving statewide office. Senator Dede Feldman and her husband Mark had taken a chance on me, an unknown, no-name candidate with no political experience. They went out of their way to give me a voice and an audience in the beautiful home that Mark built. I will never forget their early encouragement and support—both financial and moral. It meant so much to me back then that Dede, this well-respected paragon of progressive politics, saw something in me that was worth backing.

It is that memory—that summer evening—that came back to me full force as I read the pages of this memoir. And as I read, I kept asking myself how does Dede's story fit into the larger story of New Mexico politics. Who is she, anyway? An out-of-stater, progressive-before-her-time, Anglo woman from the East. A reformer. A fighter. A mentor.

You see, being a woman in electoral politics when Dede did it was tough, because there weren't many who had come before her. The organization, Emerge New Mexico, whose particular mission it is to train and run Democratic women candidates for office had not yet "emerged." The landscape for women candidates and women office holders was still uncertain. We hadn't had a woman in Congress yet, or our first woman governor, let alone more than one!

There weren't those she could look to in order to model herself as a female candidate or office holder—to show her "how it was done." For me, Dede *is* that woman who came before: the trailblazer, the way finder; one of the few that made it more possible and probable for candidates like me and countless others to succeed.

Politics in New Mexico has roots going back centuries; primaries here are often called "blood sport." With so much colonialist history, years of intergenerational trauma, battles, and revolts, New Mexico has its own unique brand of what it means to run, win, and serve.

Dede stepped into all of that with grace and a voice—like my own mother, a loud insistent voice—honed by years of journalism and tough campaigns. Though I never had the privilege of serving with her in the New Mexico State Legislature—I won my seat for the first time the same year Dede retired—I always knew her not only as a strong supporter of other ambitious female candidates, but as someone who had taken on the tough fights—prescription drug prices, health insurance, campaign finance reform—and even won some of them! I remember the newspaper articles, the photos of her alone on the floor, pressing for a tax on tobacco or transparent committee hearings, often running into a brick wall made up of the old guard, who thought they knew better. I knew her as a model, and a mentor. Someone who I looked up to and wanted to be. When Dede walks into a room—even today, though no longer in public office—people accost her in crowds to ask her opinion on this or that political topic of the day just to hear from her.

Today, as an advocate against big money in politics, Dede continues the struggle for a fairer, more equitable political system. Though no longer in the senate, she continues as a citizen reformer for the organization Common Cause, where she fights for seemingly unwinnable goals, inching ever forward toward a more just future.

Her voice is as assured and strong as ever. She continues to be a fierce campaigner, always pushing ideas before their time, never backing down. Dede is always moving forward, one step at a time.

It is my hope that this memoir will seal Dede's legacy on the list of New Mexico progressive reformers and spur a younger generation of activists to see the value in perseverance and good, old-fashioned stubbornness—no matter how many people say, "It can't be done!"

Stephanie Garcia Richard
New Mexico Commissioner of Public Lands
March 2021

I am of the opinion that my life belongs to the whole community, and as long as I live it is my privilege to do for it whatever I can. I want to be thoroughly used up when I die, for the harder I work the more I live. I rejoice in life for its own sake. Life is no 'brief candle' for me. It is a sort of splendid torch which I have got hold of for the moment, and I want to make it burn as brightly as possible before handing it on to future generations.

—George Bernard Shaw,
Man and Superman (1903)

Contents

Preface

For over a decade my office at the top of the marble staircase on the third floor of the New Mexico Capitol had been my refuge, my war room and, on the last night of each session, my bedroom. Progressive reformers had gathered there to plot and scheme with me, sitting on the couch that only committee chairs were allowed. Lobbyists had waited outside. Children had posed for photos amid the stacks of bills, files, and committee reports. The blinds were always open to the east side of the capitol where demonstrators gathered, children played on the Glenna Goodacre sculpture, and the songs of New Mexico drifted into my office.

It was time to go. The gavel had come down on the session's last motion to adjourn *sine die,* or without another day. A hush had fallen over the building, as it always did immediately after the frenzied finale in both chambers when friends and staff crowded around to hear the final congratulatory speeches. The hallways were empty save for a few stragglers making trips with boxes and bags, coming and going from their offices to the underground garage where their cars waited. The circus had left town.

I took one last look at the shelves with the row of red books holding most of New Mexico's statutes, the Medicaid handbooks, and the awards and trinkets given out by lobbyists. Margaret Garcia, my secretary, had removed the digital clock from the New Mexico Association of Health Underwriters, the fancy thermal cup from the city of Española, and the lunch sack from the Del Norte Credit Union. She had drawn the blinds and cleaned out the drawers. Gone was the script of how to introduce bills on the floor of the senate and the blank note cards with New Mexico scenes that I had used to thank members for their votes or implore them to support my bill. The walls were bare. No more enlarged cartoons, no more plaques. The huge geological map of the state of New Mexico that I had tacked up to remind me of the scale of the state I served was rolled up, along with assorted proclamations and memos. It now rested in a battered cardboard box.

Although I had told no one—and would keep the secret for another month to ensure my district would not fall into the wrong hands—I knew this was my last session. When I closed the door—once again causing the poorly attached Great Seal of the State of New Mexico to nearly fall off—I knew it would be for the last time.

Leaving elected office voluntarily, as I did in 2012, was walking away from power. I had ascended the chairmanship of an important senate committee. I had become an expert in certain fields. I had passed almost 100 bills, some of them landmarks in health and campaign finance law. Many had thanked me for doing what I did. People had prayed for me. I still have the cards, the mementos, and the little homemade gifts. There were photographs of the Rio Grande taken by an environmentalist I had helped with a bill to protect the state's rivers, student artwork from Griegos Elementary School, homemade fudge from the analyst for the Indian Affairs Committee, and a teddy bear from the New Mexico Primary Care Association.

Amid all the thank you notes and offers of congratulations, a few brave souls, my best allies, wanted to know why I would ever do such a thing. They counted on me.

It was one of the hardest things I ever did, almost as hard as winning my first election to the senate in 1996—a lifetime ago. The excitement, the game, the pure sport of the legislature was addicting. Winning and losing on a daily basis, no permanent allies, no permanent enemies. And the stakes were as high as the sky. Nothing like it.

But I am not a lifer, although I could have stayed in my safe Democratic district indefinitely, championing my progressive causes, sometimes winning and sometimes losing, looking heroic to some and villainous to others. Yet it's not healthy for democracy or elected officials themselves to stay in their posts for decades, accumulating power, becoming entrenched in their beliefs, stuck in their coalitions, and wary of innovations and change. I saw it happening all around me. The time had come to give someone with a fresh face and a new outlook a chance.

Anyway, my husband had had enough of the long absences, the phone calls, the people appearing on our porch, the sit-down dinners that went on forever, and the endless waiting for me to break away.

For years after I left, I didn't know whether I had made the right decision. I did know that, now on the outside, I had to discover what I could do on my own. I had done it before, when I came to New Mexico in the mid-1970s searching for a way to make a difference. I would do it again. There would be no quiet retirement for me. I bristled at the "happy retirement" cards I received from well-meaning constituents. They were the same ones who had thanked me profusely for my service, especially when they found out I received no salary. "I could never do what you do," they said.

Activism goes in all directions—inside, outside, off to an angle, and sideways. It comes from within, a manic desire to do something, to make peoples' lives better, to stop the worst from happening, and to find better solutions to the same old problems. I couldn't stop that even if I tried. Just like I can't stop knocking on doors, when ten more visits with voters might make the difference between victory and defeat on the endless path toward change. To that end, I've continued to communicate with friends, neighbors, and former constituents—suggesting which sheriff candidate to vote for, what to make of certain court rulings, and how to react to pandemics and impeachments. I've done it at the podium and with the pen, two tools I will not give up.

I remind people of their own power and give folks the information they need to exercise it. I do it in my blog, *A View from Just Outside the Roundhouse,* and in two books I wrote after leaving the senate. Both are instruction manuals of sorts on how to advocate for change within the system (*Inside the New Mexico Senate: Boots, Suits, and Citizens*) or create alternatives outside it (*Another Way Forward: Grassroots Solutions from New Mexico*).

For most of my political career, I'd been reminding people that they cannot be bystanders, but they must act, participate, vote, turn up in committee, run for office, or join a reform coalition as I did. I will not quit as long as there are wrongs to be righted. Since 2017, there have been plenty of wrongs to be righted. President Donald Trump's election and the daily outrages he visited on our institutions, our health, our economy, our environment, our media, on immigrants, protesters, and everyone he thought might have slighted him have spurred a new world of activism. We now hear the voices of young people, women, artists, and Native Americans. George Floyd's murder has generated even more: a nationwide uprising to promote racial justice.

It's easier than ever to fill every day with direct action, public comment, letters to elected officials, phone calls to congressional offices, media monitoring, fundraising on the web, and phone banking—and that's not even counting the new kind of electoral campaigns executed in 2020 via Zoom, text messaging, and online phone banks.

There are now more people desperate to change our country's trajectory and the civic power of ordinary citizens is growing as millennials join the political discourse. Young people are more diverse and more active than ever before.

This collection of stories traces one woman's zig-zag path to political change at the turn of the century, making my way from prim, Quaker Pennsylvania to the floor of the New Mexico Senate, where I became a champion of health care and government reform. My colonial hometown, where I was born Mary Elizabeth Whitcraft, is a long way from the quirky, diverse, and multicultural North Valley of Albuquerque. Here I honed my progressive values with a new set of adventures—reporting for an underground newspaper, going door-to-door in an ethnically mixed area, working on losing campaigns, battling local politicos, winning and losing big in the New Mexico Legislature.

Along the way I learned the importance of working from the outside as well as the inside—of being an ally as well as a player. To move the issues I cared about forward, I had to join the Democratic team and get a Hispanic community to accept me as a woman and a newcomer. Finally, I had to step forward myself as a candidate and then learn to get things done as a senator.

The journey has taken me deep into retail politics, pushing forward from one door to another, through phone calls I didn't want to make and meetings I didn't want to attend. I persevered—sometimes winning, sometimes losing.

My path has never been straight. Often it has been a defensive line against threats to gains won inch-by-inch. Sometimes it is a relentless advance toward long-sought goals like public financing or universal health care. Always it requires patience, perseverance, and an open heart. There are always ten more doors to knock on, eight more senators to persuade, and a dozen more meetings to attend.

I found many allies along my way: women struggling to come into their political own during the 1980s, idealistic students who believed in democracy, ordinary citizens disenchanted with politics as usual, and a grassroots army of liberals and environmentalists—protectors of the bosque, the Rio Grande, the cottonwoods, all those things that give the place called the North Valley its unique character.

My lesson is this: everyone, whether they know it or not, has a political contribution to make, shaped by their own experience. This contribution may be running for office. It may be advocating for an important cause. It may be starting a social enterprise to address a social problem like poverty or health inequity. It may be teaching in a classroom, being an investigative journalist, or a fundraiser. Or it may simply involve becoming a citizen in the fullest possible sense of the word—voting, keeping informed with the facts, and not always looking for easy answers.

Ten More Doors: Politics and the Path to Change is a memoir, a work of creative non-fiction dependent on memory and personal reflection. A few names have been changed to protect the innocent (and the guilty). Quotations are based on my memory of events and may not be exact. I have used contemporaneous newspaper accounts, personal notes, and my own newsletters and articles as source materials. Any mistakes are my own doing.

I owe my thanks to the many volunteers, constituents, neighbors, and allies who supported me with kindness and generosity all along the way. I apologize for sometimes not remembering everyone's exact name—but the memory of talking to extraordinary people at ordinary front doors, on porches, at street corners, or at the local supermarket will never leave me. Special thanks go to those who helped me in one way or another with this book. Some gave me ideas; others helped me assemble long-lost source materials; and still others reviewed portions of the manuscript. I am especially grateful to Stephanie Garcia Richard, Dave Barta, John Daniel, Steve Terrell, Ann Dunbar, Janet Bridges, Debbie O'Malley, Bill deBuys, Tom Udall, Susan Loubet, Viki Harrison, Barbara Baca, Michelle Otero, Pat Baca Jr., Colin Baillio, Alan Macrae, Susan Gardner, Connie Josefs, Susan Dollenger, my editor John Byram, Kelly Byram, and designer Charlie Kenesson. My biggest thanks are reserved for my husband and partner all along the way, Mark M. Feldman. We have traveled this path together. He has been there for the victories and for the defeats recounted in this book. He has supported me at every turn—including the writing of this memoir during a pandemic year like no other. I could not have done it without him.

Part I

*The personal
is political.*

—Feminist slogan, 1970

1

Taking the Leap

1995

WE HAD AGREED TO MEET AT 7:30 A.M., which was late for County Commissioner Pat Baca. The coffee at the Denny's on Coors south of the freeway was watery and the smell of hash browns blanketed the west side eatery that Pat used for his regular early morning rendezvous. This morning he was all about getting me to run for the city council.

Pat Baca was 68—almost an institution, a city father. He'd been on the city council for fifteen years under several mayors. He looked like an old-fashioned politician, with swept back gray hair, a dignified bearing, and a wry smile. I got to know him through his daughter Theresa, who ran for judge in 1986. I did a brochure for her—and voilà—I was part of the huge Baca clan. Pat and Marie had eight children—seven girls and a boy. Pat himself was one of thirteen siblings. Three brothers were the founders of Bueno Foods, the processor of green and red chile, a food that is synonymous with New Mexico. Another was a well-known Catholic priest, Father Paul.

Pat was sixty-two when he lost his biggest race to become mayor of Albuquerque in 1989 to Louis Saavedra, who everyone referred to as the "stealth mayor" because he never did or said anything. Pat had been on the city council since its formation in 1974. He'd often been the president and was the leader of a non-partisan group that created the quality of life that we now take for granted in Albuquerque with its museums and its network of open space parks like the Elena Gallegos Open Space at the foot of the Sandias.

For decades, Pat went through endless stacks of reports, attended committee hearings, coffee-and-cake reception lines, and ribbon cuttings in the rain. An elementary school principal, he gave each student a book on his or her birthday. During his mayoral campaign, we debated whether he should shave off his mustache to dispel the *patron* impression. He never did. When I was his press secretary, there was never anything outrageous to put in news releases except his constant call for an independent auditor to oversee the activities of then Mayor Ken Schultz who, many years later, was implicated in a courthouse corruption scandal. Instead, we portrayed Pat as the family man he actually was, the dedicated public servant, and the symbol of traditional civic engagement.

It was not enough. Pat was the victim of a whisper campaign that targeted him as a typical politico, a Hispanic machine politician. Election night, downtown at the La Posada Hotel, in his concession speech an angry Baca, one we had never seen before, denounced his opponent and those who spread the rumors as "racists." The old gentleman had spoken the truth. He was immediately written off as a sore loser and the consensus among those in the know was that he had no future. But he came back a year later, in 1990, winning a county commission seat.

On that cold morning, I told him I was not ready to run for office, that I had not assembled a group of supporters, didn't have enough money in the bank, and had a young daughter.

"Just get out there," he said. "Knock on doors. Let people get to know you. Apply some good old-fashioned shoe leather."

"What's the worst that could happen?" he asked.

My mind raced ahead. It had dozens of answers. I could be humiliated. I could be attacked by gangs as I went door-to-door in dangerous neighborhoods in the North Valley. My husband could divorce me; my daughter's attendance at a private school would disqualify me. My neighbors would turn against me. I'd be imprisoned for making an unintentional mistake on my campaign finance report. My best friend would run against me. I would be the subject of negative mailings—lies like those I'd seen flung against other candidates. They'd say I had DWIs or that I ate live children for breakfast.

I didn't say anything, but Pat knew what I was going through in my mind. Pat had seen his share of negative campaigning. We had been through it together and he knew what I could do.

Pat was hoping for a commitment. The man had other options, other candidates to support, and he was growing impatient.

"In the end it comes down to you and Mark going door-to-door, putting up signs, making phone calls. Ultimately, you can't count on anyone else. All I can say is that we need you in office." It was a strange, encouraging comment. Even though I had helped him in his campaign, we had been on the opposite side of almost every issue—especially, the need for a river crossing at Montaño Road.

Albuquerque's West Side had been locked in a battle with the North Valley for decades over a proposed bridge over the Rio Grande that would cut a swath through the bosque, one of the last urban riparian forests in the country. The crossing would pass through the heart of the North Valley and destroy hundreds of aging cottonwood trees. For years, along with other North Valley residents, I had attended rowdy hearings before the Environmental Planning Commission, testified before the Mid-Region Traffic Planning Board, written letters to the editor about nominations to the National Historic Register, given money at fundraisers for lawsuits, protested decisions made by the city administration, and even demonstrated against the bridge.

So, when Pat Baca, considered by bridge opponents to be THE enemy, suggested I run for office, I took it very seriously. It would be months before I acted.

When I thought about running for office I saw my potential supporters as members of the groups I had helped, or reported on—environmental advocates, women, candidates and their supporters, progressives I knew from ProPAC (a progressive political action committee), the American Civil Liberties Union, the Women's Political Caucus, and other people I considered part of a larger movement for change. We call them "progressives" now, but then they were just friends with whom I had been in the trenches. But still, I hesitated. It's one thing to help others take the leap, but it's entirely another to offer up your own reputation, energy, and time.

And then, suddenly, a light bulb went off in my head.

~

The decision came as I turned onto Lomas Boulevard. I had just emerged from the city's underground parking lot, a concrete bomb shelter of a place, whose spooky dark rows of cars led to a nondescript door which gives way to the Albuquerque City Council chambers. It was hardly a grand entrance to arguably the most important building in this city of almost 400,000 (now 560,000).

I had passed through that door and departed from the latest meeting of the city council, then grappling with the rapid growth of the city, the inadequate transportation system, and the issue that brought it all to a head: a bridge across the river and through the bosque in my neighborhood. The shouting matches and the lawsuits were over. The long-delayed vote had been taken. Opponents of the bridge were outnumbered; our city councilor, Vince Griego, had been powerless to stop it.

It was getting dark, but as I headed home, I could still see the trusty old Leonard Tire and Automotive Repair Shop and, from a distance, the gray county courthouse. I thought about the city council's formal, drab proceedings—the unimaginative debate, the predictable outcome, and the incumbents who had held their seats for decades. I knew I could do better—if I had the chance.

But I had never had a chance to become a leader. There was no way in. Sure, I had campaigned for the local Democrats and was the ward chair for Ward 11A. But I wasn't hand-picked by the insiders. I hadn't sucked up to the business crowd or been ruthless enough in climbing the party ladder. I was too liberal, too Anglo, too educated, and too female for my part of town—the Democratic heartland. Most of the office holders had been born and bred here. Neighborhoods like Los Griegos bore their family names. They went to Valley High School and were members of San Felipe de Neri or Our Lady of Guadalupe churches. I had just arrived here—20 years ago.

~

To heck with it! I would do it anyway. I had my husband's blessing. He knew the odds, but he knew me, too, and knew that politics in one way or another was part of my makeup, whether it was writing articles, protesting the war in college, or pushing my causes—the environment, women, and people with disabilities. We had gone over all this.

Now was the time. A popular referendum had limited the terms of city councilors and the incumbent would be ineligible, leaving a rare open seat—or so I thought at the time. An appeals court later overturned the election and the longtime incumbents held on for another decade. By the time the court acted, however, I was already walking the streets, firm in my decision.

My friends tried, for the most part, to talk me out of it. The progressives and the women used to defeat, were cautious. The savvy ones did not believe an Anglo could win in a Hispanic district. Dave Duhigg, a friend who had helped so many progressive Democrats, sat down with me at Java Joe's, a funky new café that catered to the downtown crowd with bagels, artwork by unknown locals, lattes, and mocha java. We put pencil to paper and talked money.

"How much do you think you can raise?" he asked.

I didn't know.

"How much could you put in of your own money?"

I didn't know. I'd have to talk to Mark.

"Okay. Make a list of ten friends who will give you at least 100 dollars," he asked. "If you can't do that, it's hopeless."

I came up with eight. I realized how hard it would be to ask.

It was a sobering conversation.

But Ann Dudley Edwards, Geri Lingo, Mary Dudley, Sally Dehon, and others from a women's group that had gathered regularly to support one another during the late'80s, all encouraged me. Julie Dunleavy, Mary Kirschner. and other friends from the New Mexico Press Women organization were ready to help. But unlike the members of Emerge, the Democratic women's group, which later began to prep women candidates in fundraising, targeting, and the fine points of campaigning, my friends knew little of the mechanics of politics, but they gave me the confidence I needed.

Hadn't Pat Baca suggested a path—just going for it—knocking on doors, ringing doorbells, introducing yourself, and asking for the support of your neighbors? True, they were mostly Hispanic, but his family had adopted me, after all. Sure, the political pundits said that ethnic voting—where voters from one ethnic group always voted for candidates of the same background—usually determined election outcome. But, they always said, that was only if voters had no other information about the candidates. There was the glimmer of hope.

And so, I began.

There were lots of obstacles in this, my first campaign. And they started soon enough at the city clerk's annex, where election records were kept.

~

Aurelia Sanchez, Tomas Lucero, Faustino Zamora, James Baca, Cordelia Lovato, Eloy Maldonado, Rupita Tafoya.

I dutifully input the names and addresses from Precinct 152 into my Macintosh computer. It was an early model, too clunky to load easily into the back seat of my old Subaru for the trip down to the city clerk's annex, a nondescript box I had never noticed before near the corner of Menaul and 6th Street. There, inside the box, beneath the fluorescent lights, workers were silently inputting registration data from elections past, filing old signature sheets and absentee ballots. They were shocked to see me.

I was attempting what no one else did then. I was collecting the names of the people who actually voted in the last city council election. Candidates can now do this with ease. They simply order the file from the city clerk—signed, sealed and ready for pick up.

But this was 1995. It was a tedious, two-person task in which one person read the names and data for each voter from the signature roster used at each polling place on election day, and the other input it into a database.

I was the "Little Engine that Could," though. I wanted to be on the Albuquerque city council.

By the end of the afternoon, we had counted twenty-four Griegos, ten Martinezes, and seven Sanchezes. I didn't find anyone other than my husband with the last name of Feldman in Precinct 152 or any of the other precincts in the North Valley area that I wanted to represent. Tony Lucero, Al Serrano, Tito Chavez, Vince Griego, Ed Sandoval—these were the guys who held office, brought home the bacon, and stayed put, for decade after decade, in the house, the senate, the council, and the commission.

Now I knew why.

"Get real, you won't even make a dent," my computer buddy Jim told me as he looked at the names on the list of voters.

"Face it, you're not from here, you're not a Catholic, you don't have a big family, and you don't have a Hispanic last name."

All true. I had moved into the area in 1976, an Anglo in a working-class neighborhood. I had never felt like an outsider until now. My neighbors had helped me lay adobes.

I had the foolish belief that voters could look beyond ethnicity, gender, and place of birth. And now, with my revolutionary method of targeting the right voters in a small universe, I had social science on my side. No one else was doing it.

Still, I suffered the hidden doubt of the true believer, the idealist, and the religious convert. New Mexico, after all, is drawn on a multicultural map. It is a majority minority state, where no one ethic group has a majority. Hispanics comprise approximately 48% of the population, Whites 37%, Native Americans 11%, Blacks 2.6%, and Asians 1.8%.

And history has its consequences. Memories of occupation and oppression do not die easily. Faustino Zamora's family lost its ranch up north because it couldn't afford the property taxes. James Baca's grandmother died on the long march back to the reservation from the Bosque Redondo.

Campaigns are based on stereotypes, on superficial markers, on races and names. It is a matter of assembling votes and putting blocks together to build a temporary house for a majority.

I would just have to see for myself. It would be a journey. First, let me knock on the doors of people like Faustino Holguin, Cordelia Lovato, and Eloy Maldonado to see what they think.

2

Uganda

July 1972

I STOOD ON THE DIRT FLOOR ASKING THE STUDENTS, "What does the English word 'power' mean to you?" The students, most of them taller than me, were in their early teens. It was their world—the Haibale School in Fort Portal, Uganda. They were all boys who wore blue shorts and white shirts with collars. They had bare feet so calloused that it looked like the students were wearing shoes. There were no desks, only a blackboard, a roof covered with corrugated tin, and the smoothed blocks that formed the gray walls.

I suppose it was an unfair question from a young white teacher from America here only for the summer. No matter how much she and her husband, Mr. Mark, were helping to build a new classroom, she would never understand.

The 14-year-olds were polite. They were the cream of the crop, those whose parents could afford the uniform and the modest school fees. Where they would go after this was any-one's guess. It was Idi Amin's Uganda in the early 1970s. The reign of terror was just beginning.

A hand shot up from the back of the small group, then another, and another.

"It is force," a clear British voice said, without hesitation. "It is like when you cut a piece of wood in half."

"It is when you are a leader, then you have power," said another.

"Power to do what?" I asked.

"Power to do anything," he replied.

"Like what," I insisted.

"To go away. To go in the army. To kill other people, to sell your wife," he said.

"How does a leader get such power?" I asked, thinking about how to boil down all the political theory I had studied at the university, the various sources of authority—heredity, election, divine right, and charisma.

Here it was in real life, an issue that existed only in the abstract before. My high school students at George School, a privileged, Quaker prep school in Pennsylvania, had dis-cussed it many times. Theirs was a world where absolute power was limited, decisions were shared, and elections were held. They knew they had voices and rights.

"He takes it," said the student.

The answer was simple. It was a matter of brute force. Years of British colonialism had taught them about that.

"But what about the chief, the tribe?" I asked, treading on uncertain ground.

"That's different," they said, without any explanation.

"That's not the army. That's not rifles or machetes."

Time was running out. Before long we would have to return to our mutual task, laying up the blocks that would form the walls of their new classroom that our work camp was building.

There was so much I wanted to ask. So much I wondered about the citizens of this new, small nation of red dirt roads and swaying banana trees where people wore T-shirts silk-screened with photos of their leader.

"Do the people themselves have any power?" I asked, almost embarrassed, almost afraid that someone was listening, someone from Kampala, the capital.

The question itself was a luxury.

Silence. These were only children, I persuaded myself. The same children that only a few years later would be drafted into brutal child militias like the Lord's Resistance Army, who would be engaged in genocide, who would cross borders, kidnap other children, and who would die of AIDS.

"Sometimes we can make things a little better," one ventured. "We can get an education. We can get money."

"But everything is dangerous," said another.

~

Later that summer the danger became palpable. An order had gone out from the capital that foreigners were not to be trusted. Hippies were not welcome. Beards were outlawed, so were miniskirts, which were interpreted to be any skirt that didn't touch the ground. I shuddered to think how we would get the high school students we had brought with us on this Peace Corps-style work camp to take the order seriously. Mark immediately shaved his beard. The three boys on our crew didn't have to worry. They were too young. The girls—all seven of them—were willing. They saw a fashion opportunity. They bought African cloth and wrapped their young hips, sarong style, just like the African girls at Kinya-maseka Teacher Training College where they were staying in the dorm.

Our work camp could not have come at a worse time. Idi Amin was consolidating the coup that brought him to pow-er. Opponents—even many inside his own circle—were killed brutally, their corpses displayed on the front pages of newspapers. The day after the order about the beards, Amin encouraged the people to take matters into their own hands when they saw anyone violating his new laws.

The mob had been empowered.

It was hard to keep a low profile in our zebra stripped minibus, but we did our best, thinking that we were so far away from the capital in Fort Portal, near Zaire, that no one would pay us any mind. (We later learned that our arrival had been broadcast on the radio.) After all, the whole town had welcomed us as their new friends from America—the teachers and students who were going to work alongside the Ugandan students—to do what their school principal, George Bagamba, had been planning for years and build a new classroom. Bagamba himself probably had no more than a high school education but he knew what he was doing. For months, he'd been assembling materials—cement blocks, the lumber from the Rwenzori Mountains, bags of cement, and nails. The parents contributed and somehow George had found the money for the relatively expensive building mate-rials. Now he had the last ingredient—the skilled labor to put it all together in a short period of time.

My husband Mark, then an elementary school teacher, became the head of the construction crew. The students jokingly called him "*bwana*." He had never built anything. His only training came two weeks before when a fellow teacher taught him how to lay out a building so it would be square and how to use a level so the walls would not be lopsided or wavy. Once there, he learned quickly. By the end of our stay Mr. Mark, as he would be called, had developed the skills that would propel him into a career of home building in New Mexico, using adobe bricks not so different from the cement ones we used in Fort Portal.

~

Every day before we began our work, the whole school—teachers and students—would gather in a circle to sing and dance for us. There would be speeches, thank yous and prayers for success, all in a flurry of students in purple uniforms. Most of the children were too young for building but they had small gifts of fruit and crafts for us. Once they separated the big stones from the little ones, which we used in the foundation. The work was hot and backbreaking, but progress was quick. The cement was watered down. We had no mixer, but we did the best we could with buckets.

The American students made it fun, with games and stunts that drew in the curious African kids. The Africans were getting to know the Americans; the Americans were getting to know the Africans. Joy Bright, one of our students, walked three miles through the bush with one of the students and joined a family meal at her home. She came back with a chicken.

At night we shopped for canned goods, meat, tuna fish, noodles—anything to fill the stomachs of hungry teenagers.

We were warned about eating fresh vegetables, but the lure of the market was too much. Cautioned against drinking the water, we guzzled warm Fantas, and ate more green bananas than we could ever have imagined. Both went well with peanut butter, which was our staple. In the process of shopping, we met the butcher, the grocers, and the clerks at the bank where we exchanged money. They were glad to have our business.

Midway through our stay a new order came down. All Asians were ordered to leave the country in three months. They could only take the equivalent of $200 dollars per person with them. Their properties would be repossessed, and we later found out, distributed to favored military men.

This was the whole middle class of the developing country—between 50-70,000 people. The Indians were the shopkeepers, the traders, the card clubs, and the shandy drinkers. The families were the descendants of workers the British had brought to the colony to build the railroad and other infrastructure projects. They were English speakers; they were educated. And now they were nothing. Within a few months they would be refugees in Canada, in England, or in America. The whole community panicked. They were giving away their possessions to friends, contacting relatives in India or Australia, and giving us, their new customers and friends, their money, their saris, and their jewelry. Now I knew what it must have been like as Jews scrambled to leave Eastern Europe in the late 1930s.

We were nearing the end of our project at Haibale— framing up the trusses to support the roof, then lifting the beams into place. But there was a problem. Mark was sick. He was dizzy and in bed. It was dysentery. Not to worry, they said, everyone gets it here.

Then what? He was bwana, the captain of the building crew. There was only one answer. Mrs. Bwana would have to lead. The Africans were dubious, but there was no choice. That last day, I was the foreman of the building crew. Little Johnson, George's brother, had left for another job. Dave Hedden, the 14-year-old Texan with a cowboy hat, and George Bagamba came through with the heavy lifting, with the girls—now stronger than ever—wielding hammers, fastening the sides, and straightening the beams.

Mark got better and returned to his role as the crew leader. But for me things were never the same. I knew I could do it, and so could seven other all-American girls, who provided the bulk of the workforce, built classrooms, sang songs, and learned that theirs was not the only way.

The projects finished, we made it over the border to Tanzania. Travel was hazardous. Our whereabouts were monitored and sometimes announced over the radio. We never traveled at night. Every checkpoint was a nightmare of worry, sometimes lasting hours. The students' parents knew more than we did, and they had been contacting George School. The American press had begun to pick up on the atrocities that were happening in Africa. A Peace Corps volunteer had been kidnapped.

Before Uganda I never knew the feel of a dictatorship—the fear, the sense of powerlessness that enveloped everyone, including young students who had once dreamed of a better future, including an education that unlocked doors and put food in distended bellies. I was a privileged American, naïve enough to believe that the revolution was at hand, that young people had the power to stop a war in Vietnam and change the world.

I was just then emerging from the Age of Aquarius, where harmony and understanding prevailed and idealism reigned. By 1972, the taste of the sixties was still in my mouth and the memories of Woodstock fresh. In San Francisco, I had smoked my fair share of weed, spaced out with the Grateful Dead, and braved the San Francisco police to protest the invasion of Cambodia.

The Ugandan situation made all of that look juvenile. The contrast between the US in the early 1970s and Uganda was striking. And there was worse to come. By the end of Amin's reign of terror, some estimate that 300,000 were dead. Victims of Amin's forces were often abducted, told to take off their shoes, and get in the trunk of the police car. They were never heard from again, but their shoes lined the roads.

I told our students that I would kiss the ground when we landed at JFK Airport in New York. The responsibility of leading a group of teenagers through the dangerous country—just to do a good deed—had been huge. For the whole plane trip back, I thought about our narrow escape.

Something inside me had shifted. I realized that it was possible to lose your country, your future to brutality or dictatorship. Coups were possible. Bad guys could overthrow institutions and use the military to punish enemies of a different religion, tribe, or race. They could even throw out a country's entire middle class. We saw it happen right before our very eyes.

I knew then what it must have felt like in the 1930s in Europe as Hitler was gaining power.

What stuck with me was the powerlessness. A few in Fort Portal, Uganda, namely George Bagamba, had dared to make a difference, making an alliance with another school in another land, trying to lift his community up with better

19

education and a new classroom. Most had no experience in self-government and no idea that they could change things as individuals or as citizens of a nation or a state. Their lives were at the mercy of larger forces.

Yet there were blocks to build with—a history shared through song and dance, a hospitable, generous nature, a curiosity, and smiles that could not be extinguished. The sound of the drum from afar, the tribe, the town center where generations had gathered, traded, and sat smoking on overturned cans. These things are indelible. I know now there is strength in them, just as there is strength in the chiming of church bells in Albuquerque's North Valley, the smell of green chile roasting, the piñon smoke, and the snow falling on the plaza in Old Town.

In the years since we left Fort Portal with its red dirt roads, swaying banana trees, and neat rows of tea bushes, I've wondered what happened to the little schoolhouse we built on the hillside 48 years ago and the community we discovered there. We lost touch with George Bagamba and Little Johnson. The folded, blue tissue paper airmail stopped coming. I wondered if AIDS or war ended their stories.

It was just the beginning of mine. My injustice radar had been turned on, along with a new sense of pragmatism. I went back to teaching at George School determined in my own work to make sure it couldn't happen here. I never dreamed that this determination would last and propel me into politics. I knew only that young people needed to learn the history of countries like Uganda, to pay attention to what they read in the newspaper, to the ongoing war in Vietnam, to the peace plans, and the scandals. It was a prerequisite for intelligent activism.

~

Today's version of the Quaker work camp we led is AmeriCorps, Teach for America, the Job Corps, and in New Mexico, the Rocky Mountain Youth Corps, on whose board I serve. The American Friends Service Committee introduced the model in the 1930s, long before it was adapted for the Peace Corps in the 1960s. These programs combine the best of community service and hands-on learning where work, direct experience, and exposure to different kinds of cultures replaces more traditional education. Participants begin to recognize that diversity is strength. The programs give me hope in a divided nation where many are isolated in their familiar bubbles.

Looking back, I wonder about the naivete of the 1972 African work camp we led as 25-year-olds. We took responsibility for ten young lives—our students. It was dangerous, almost reckless. The students were tough and resilient but still they were privileged American teenagers and we were not that different from them. Yet we all rose to the occasion. We built two classrooms, learned a little Swahili, ate bananas, and came to understand what growing up in a post-colonial world felt like. We experienced the sacrifices families made to educate their children, and then, what a dictatorship meant for young people facing the future, like those boys I taught in the classroom as I stood on that dirt floor.

3

Miss Mayflower

August 1955

It was a family road trip, 1955 style, powering down Route 66 from Chicago south and west to arrive, ironically, in Albuquerque's North Valley, the area I represented in the New Mexico Senate 40 years later. My father, a newspaperman, and my mother, the epitome of an elementary school teacher, had been talking about "the West" forever. Now that we had our brand new, two-tone, 1955 Plymouth station wagon, we were ready to set off from the colonial suburbs of Philadelphia for the purple mountains majesty. We followed the AAA TripTik to the national parks, determined to camp out of the back of our stylish new wagon. My mother brought her Bisquick and the *Better Homes and Gardens New Cook Book* so we could make pancakes over the open fire.

We did it all, traveling from Lake Michigan, where we stayed on a sailboat owned by a war buddy of my father's, to Zion, Bryce, Yellowstone, and the rim of the Grand Canyon—me, staring endlessly at the green and white woven ceiling inside the Plymouth, looking for the next Stuckey's, my father, a history buff, going on endlessly about Lewis and Clark, Teddy Roosevelt, and the WPA. I was in fourth grade. I was constantly nagging my parents to hurry up and get to California, and, if not, to stop at every swimming pool along the route.

We found one at the Casa Grande Lodge near Old Town in Albuquerque. It was a typical Route 66 motor court with people so friendly that we stayed extra days, exploring the petroglyphs, eating this funny green stuff they called chile, and making side trips to Santa Fe and Taos. We ate at the Hacienda Restaurant and my mother bought me a fringed buckskin jacket in Old Town that I wore almost every day for almost two years afterward regardless of the weather.

The West did not disappoint. The sense of exploration and adventure, the outdoors, and the brilliant blue sky were stuck in the back of my mind.

I went on with my young life, riding my Schwinn bike past the grange outside of my hometown, West Chester, Pennsylvania. It was still a small town, the county seat, not yet just another Philadelphia suburb. Sometimes I would venture as far as the Birmingham Friends meetinghouse, to the open fields where, in 1777, General George Washington had fought General William Howe in one of the bloodiest battles of the Revolutionary War, the Battle of Brandywine. I went to strawberry festivals, ran to the corner drugstore for ice cream, walked in the shade along Price Street to the movie theater, and sat with my grandmother in rocking chairs with rush seats made at the local prison. A Quaker, she still used the "plain language." "Thee doesn't do that, does thee?" she would ask if I was caught chewing gum.

The milkman still delivered milk in his windowless truck; the egg man came right to your door with his basket. I went with my parents to auctions on farms, wandered through old kitchens with crocks, and played with butter churns from the nearby Pennsylvania Dutch country. Even before college, I had majored in Americana. I grew up with my parents' love of antiques. Almost instinctively, I knew the worth of an arrow back Windsor chair or a piece of Delft.

History formed a low, gray ceiling, which hung over the handsome brick houses of my town, popping up suddenly at the Civil War monuments with rose bushes kept up by the ladies auxiliaries. The Historical Society, which in my teenage years, I dubbed the "Hysterical Society," was important and authoritative. It recorded that the Friends meetinghouse where my family sat in silence on long benches was built in 1821. It affirmed that my ancestors served in the Continental Army and endured the winter at Valley Forge. It documented the stops along the Underground Railroad run by Quaker schools in the area.

I caught only glimpses of the other side of West Chester where Puerto Ricans, Blacks, and Mexicans who worked in the mushroom houses nearby lived, literally, on the other side of the tracks. Later, I would learn that a true hero, Bayard Rustin, a civil rights organizer and a co-author of Martin Luther King's speech at the March on Washington, was among them.

Finally, sometime after my trip west, I suddenly felt stifled, bored with the age of it all, the gentility of the front porches, the taste of the ham loaf at the covered-dish supper, even the predictable beauty of green trees overhanging the sidewalks. I couldn't breathe. I was bored—an only child, with nothing to do but hang around with old people. Even my name seemed stale: Mary Elizabeth Whitcraft. It was from another century, a combination of the first names of my grandmothers, Elizabeth Davis, a Quaker schoolteacher, and Mary McCloud, a Scottish immigrant. And it was too long, too waspy. I might just as well be "Miss Mayflower."

And then something odd happened, the summer before I entered seventh grade in a new school. It happened in Hershey, Pennsylvania, where my family was attending the annual pre-season football game featuring my father's *alma mater,* Gettysburg College. He was gung ho. We went every year. It was 1958 and cheerleaders were unimaginably important. They were popular, peppy, and all grown up in a wonderful world I wanted to be part of. In that stadium, one of the girls yelling, "Go G-Burg! Push 'em back, shove 'em back—waay back," was a girl named Dede. I spotted her immediately. She was cute. The other girls crowded around her. I wanted to be just like her. I decided then and there that I was Dede, not Mary Elizabeth. I announced my decision to my parents, practiced saying Dede Whitcraft a few times, and that was that. A month later, I entered my new school and simply announced myself as Dede. No one was the wiser. I have been Dede ever since.

I am embarrassed every time I tell the story. A cheerleader? At least I could have chosen a nickname that remotely made sense, say Mimi or Mamie. But none of that. No more Miss Mayflower. I was going for the total transformation. And it stuck. I had a new school, a new name, and a new persona. I had broken with the past, with my family's tradition. It would not be the last time that I reinvented myself.

~

The first time I left that old world was in 1969, after college, when my new husband, Mark Feldman, a city boy, took me far away, to San Francisco. I had married young, and like my parents before me, I set out in a station wagon for California. This time I made it, landing in a new world a few years after the 1967 Summer of Love. We listened to the Grateful Dead—before they were superstars—in high school auditoriums, explored the coastline at Golden Gate Park, and went to nude beaches. We marched against the Cambodian invasion, ate Chinese food, smoked marijuana, took acid, and questioned everything. I can still smell the eucalyptus and see a glimpse of blue sky breaking through the fog. Yet we knew we were not permanent settlers and returned to our Pennsylvania roots for jobs as teachers in schools run by the same Society of Friends I knew so well.

New Mexico was different. We came here in 1975 with an intention to learn from traditions that were not our own, in search of alternatives to the mainstream, to explore, to design new kinds of dwellings, and to start afresh. We had heard about the geodesic domes and the communes in Placitas and Drop City. We had read about them in the *Whole Earth Catalog.* Mark was enrolled in the University of New Mexico Architecture School, then a hotbed of innovation and passive solar pioneers. The words "appropriate technology" dripped from our mouths, and the romance of building our own house from mud and stones shoved us forward.

That first summer we went everywhere, lured by the sky, the space, the smell of rain somewhere in the distance. Months earlier, it would never have occurred to us to drive down a dirt road at top speed, windows open, pine trees whizzing by, birds flying above. The weather could change at any minute. Hail could fall. Dust devils arise. The possibilities were endless.

There were dances at the pueblos, national forests, tribal rodeos, pre-historic sites, and so much to explore. But after that...then what? I would have to find some way to earn the money to build our house and carve out some kind of career. I didn't really have a plan. Maybe if I just kept exploring, something would come my way. In September, I took a job at the Horseman's Kitchen at the New Mexico State Fair. I got up early to serve coffee to jockeys from Mexico who took their coffee *con crema*. I learned about quarter horses. I tried in vain to understand the West Texas accent that the owners and trainers used to order chicken-fried steak. It was a different culture, one of many that this strange new land had to offer.

I wanted to dive in. I signed up for a Spanish course and swore I would never mispronounce "Juan Tabo" or "Gila." I was the outsider, not vice versa. We had exciting new teachers—young do-it-yourselfers, radical journalists, Native American activists, all willing to show us the lay of the land. Most of all, we wanted to dig into the earth, to find a home base, someplace where we could build a house of our own, one that combined tradition and innovation, not just on paper, but built with our hands, using the strength of our backs, shooting up from the new energy we felt from our big break with the East Coast. Then everything else would fall into place.

We scoured the neighborhoods—looking for run-down houses that could be "retrofit" to become passive solar haciendas, with brick floors and adobe walls to absorb the heat from skylights and southern windows. Somehow, we gravitated to the North Valley. The prices were cheaper and there was good New Mexican food. Every Saturday we ate huevos rancheros at El Camino and the Mexican Kitchen. There, we listened to local residents greet one another, *"Buenos días, señor."* We heard mothers calling their children, *"mijita,"* and mourning with them, *"qué lástima,"* when things didn't go well. We went up and down 4th Street so many times that we knew what time St. Therese let out and where the buses stopped in Alameda.

For the most part, realtors in 1976 avoided showing Anglo newcomers properties in the North and South Valley. The area was too mixed, not only between commercial, industrial, and residential, but between Anglos and Hispanics. You never knew when there might be a broken-down truck in the next yard, a pack of barking dogs, or overstuffed couches on the front porch. Buyers from the Midwest preferred the Heights with the more homogenous neighborhoods built after the war by Dale Bellamah or Sam Hoffman. It was easier to shop at the new strip malls lining the nearby avenues, named Juan Tabo, Eubank, and Louisiana. The crime rate was lower there, we were told, and property values were more secure than in the Valley areas, which had long been used by Hispanic farmers as fields for alfalfa, beans, chile, and corn.

We were not deterred. We were in our late 20s, eager to become New Mexicans. We liked the gritty reality that the Midwesterners rejected. We loved the cornfield across from 1821 Meadow View Drive, where the house we eventually bought was located. The mix, the Hispanic population, and the unpredictability of it all, lured us to the Valley as if we were caught in some kind of magnetic field.

It couldn't be more different than the streets of West Chester, Pennsylvania—the prim lawns, the orderly rows of veteran row houses, the white columns and front porches. In the North Valley, the house numbers were not even sequential, and the landscaping was irregular. A magnificent territorial adobe with Greek revival windows might stand next to a shattered stucco box, with only dirt and trash in the front yard. On some streets, strange black birds with split tails chattered among themselves, or pigs snorted from the backyard. Then suddenly a house made entirely of brazenly colored tiles would appear, or an exquisite handmade iron gate.

The Casa Grande Lodge, where my parents and I had stayed 30 years earlier, was still there in nearby Old Town when we moved in. It was only blocks away from our new house. Mark and I ate dinner there almost every night the summer we rebuilt and solarized our new house. It smelled like ammonia. The pool was closed and there was a drive-up liquor window that I hadn't remembered from years before. The Casa Grande was not so grand anymore. Its owners were East Indians, refugees from East Africa, another irony. A few years earlier we had witnessed the wholesale eviction of Asians from Uganda on the orders of Idi Amin. Some had settled along old Route 66.

4

Tortilla Windows

June 1976

THE SOUNDS OF THE PARTY OUTSIDE OUR BEDROOM window that June night were pleasant at first, but then someone turned up the amplifier. The tired Kingsmen classic, "Louie, Louie," flooded our new neighborhood. "Louie Louie, oh no, you take me where ya gotta go, yeah, yeah, yeah, baby." The voices rose and then, the unmistakable sound of bottles smashing against concrete. The gunshots came in twos, then fours. The music suddenly stopped, and the beer-soaked crowd dispersed. The dogs continued to howl, pleading for help until the North Valley Area Command arrived on the scene. The Valley High School graduation party was over and so was our first night on Meadow View Drive.

We had bought our small adobe house off Rio Grande Boulevard in the North Valley without spending the night there, secure in our "research," which consisted mainly of driving up and down 4th Street and eating in all the Mexican restaurants. We were drawn to this unpretentious area of the city, its mixture of people and houses, and its surprises. We spent a lot of time dreaming about the passive solar greenhouse we would build on the south side of our small, plain house to provide fresh vegetables and heat to warm our immigrant bones. But nothing prepared us for our first night. All at once, the reality of this mixed-income, multi-ethnic area appeared in stark relief.

Our first tip-off should have been the dogs—the terriers, the chihuahuas, the rottweilers, the mangy shepherds, the chows, the retrievers, and last but not least, the pit bulls. They were going berserk, emitting a cacophony of sharp barks, high pitched yips, low snarls, and contagious howls. You could hear them throwing themselves against the chain link fences that outlined the yards near us.

Or maybe it should have been our next-door neighbors, the Lovatos, from whom we bought our land and the small, crooked house that stood upon it. The Lovato sons had a proclivity for pit bulls, beer, women, cock fighting, and Harley Davidsons.

The contrast between my old world and the new one could not have been starker.

I come from stone barns, Quaker meetinghouses, and straight-backed chairs. Our neighbors had quiet porches where they rocked back and forth on uniform white rockers. There were no couches outside, and the cars were hidden back in the alley. An N.C. Wyeth painting hung in my high school cafeteria. When I attended college in Pennsylvania, I walked right by a statue of Benjamin Franklin every day on my way to class.

The families we knew had last names like Sharpless, Hoopes, Smedley, and Matlock. History loomed large. There were no Griegos, Luceros, Candelarias, or Trujillos. My own neighborhood was orderly, predictable, and homogeneous. I see now that it was actually segregated, not legally of course, but in fact (de facto). There were few blacks or Puerto Ricans in our neighborhood. They lived, literally, on the other side of the tracks.

New Mexico had a different narrative than the ones I had studied in school. I never heard about the Spanish in the Southwest or the Pueblo Revolt. Somehow the history books skipped over the indelicacies of Western expansion. Once I arrived here, I realized, the melting pot never quite melted. People spoke different languages, ate pork or lamb roasted overnight in a pit dug in the ground, partied at *matanzas,* danced in cowboy boots, and went to Mass at the church the next morning. In the North Valley, Hispanic, Native American, Anglo, Irish, and Italian families intermarried. Sometimes, as I found out later as I walked door-to-door looking for votes, there was a sign over the door introducing the family as the "Los MacDonalds." My mother's Scotts ancestors would have been proud of the mix—and the tolerance that the sign signified.

Our chosen land was exciting. It was different. From the start, I wanted in.

Building our house ourselves was the ticket. We bought a 1955 one-ton Chevy truck (immediately raising our status in the eyes of the neighbors), hauled gravel, dug trenches, knocked down walls, raised roofs for clerestories, and mixed mud with hoes in a giant volcano in our front yard. Our neighbors, who had been wondering what these crazy gringos were up to, began to stop their cars, get out, ask

questions and offer advice about the details that now preoc-
cupied us. We had questions like whether the original *terrone*
blocks could be salvaged, whether they should be plastered or
exposed, or whether we really needed gringo blocks around
the doorways. We wondered how we would scrape off the
bark from the *lattias* that we had gathered in the Jemez so
they would be smooth like the ones we had seen in Santa Fe.
Our neighbors knew.

They were a practical, hard-working lot, we found. By day,
many worked for the city or the state. Some were employees
of the US Post Office. By night and on the weekends, they
were do-it yourselfers, busy keeping gardens, laying adobes,
irrigating their fields, sometimes even traveling back and
forth to northern New Mexico to keep up the ranch. And
heaven help you if you threatened the land, or the place that
they called home. They were prepared to defend their turf.
I would find out years later just how prepared, as I joined a
decades-long struggle that citizens had waged against the
construction of a bridge over the Rio Grande through the
nearby bosque, one of the last urban riparian forests in the
United States. The struggle brought together newcomers
and traditional families—Hispanic and Anglo—who loved
the quirky, mixed rural-urban lifestyle in the North Valley.
It involved lawsuits, raucous hearings before the Environmental Planning Commission, appeals to the Mid-Region
Traffic Planning Board, nominations to the National Historic
Register, fundraisers, transportation studies, scuffles with the
city administration, demonstrations, anger, and sadness as
the Mayor chopped down a treasured cottonwood tree at the
intersection of Rio Grande and Montaño.

By the time the bridge battle was lost in 1996, the motley
crew of Hispanics, along with a new group of young families,

artists, and liberals (like me) who had been attracted to the Valley had become a band of savvy activists who knew the power of letters to the editor, of numbers, of contributions, of testimony, of stories, and of history. They were now battle tested and on high alert to preserve the character of the traditional neighborhoods, the open spaces, and the human scale that defined the place they loved. I had become one of them.

That was all to come, though, on our first night in the Valley. But I should have known that the call of community would sound for me, as it does for citizens everywhere. Years ago, my Eastern ancestors had shed blood to defend their turf in the Revolutionary War. Later my relatives attended public meeting after public meeting, raised money for the schools, ran for local office, served on the board of the Society for the Prevention of Cruelty to Animals. My great aunt was the county clerk at a time when women were not in government. She wore a hat and sensible shoes and walked to work. My grandfather ran for county treasurer. He lost.

Even as my hometown turned into a suburb that featured colonial replicas and reproductions of all things historic, the citizens were willing to fight—to keep Burger Kings out of the neighborhood or to preserve a favorite marsh or an open field from development. The impulse is universal. Whether it is New Mexico or Pennsylvania, concerned citizens will defend their turf and try to make it better.

~

As for the violence, our first night in the North Valley turned out to be an aberration. "It was nothing," Mike, the graduate from across the street, said the next day. "We were just having some fun." Our next-door neighbors turned out to be our best allies, helping us build an adobe wall between our two properties, introducing us to pick-and-shovel building that first summer. Celia, the family's matriarch, insisted that we put small windows in the solid wall providing privacy for both our properties. "Tortilla windows" she called them—for passing tortillas in emergencies.

Every morning at 5:30 a.m. the smell of Celia's bacon and, in the winter, her wood fire drifted over the chain link fence surrounding her front yard. It was like clockwork. We would hear the sounds of her sons' motley fleet of old trucks warming up before their staggered morning departures. Then a van from the Senior Center would sound its horn. A city worker would rattle the gate, bearing meals on wheels. A chorus of dogs from up and down the street would begin baying, and Celia would make her way out, a cigarette drooping from her lips, swing back the gate and open the yard for the morning.

For years after our house was built, Celia rode herd over her grown sons, who came and went, occasionally hanging out with us, smoking cigarettes or drinking beer as we watched traffic go by or talked about the latest scandal at city hall. Mostly though, we went our separate ways. Sometimes a police car would appear next door at the curb, and one of the brothers would come out of the house to deal with the problem. The neighbors had begun to complain about the barking dogs, the smell of horses in the back, or the constant noise of motorcycles revving up before their roaring departure.

While other neighbors complained, we kept our silence— maintaining the bond Celia and I had established that first summer. Our code was to never complain about your neighbor unless you speak to him first. The philosophy saw us through seasons of cockfighting, generations of pit bulls, and scores of late-night parties. The smell of pigs was once a problem for clients arriving at Mark's finally renovated studio. It's not what you expect in the heart of the city. They belonged to another neighbor, Val Lucero, and we tolerated them just like the Luceros and the Lovatos had tolerated us earlier, making messes all over our front yard, mixing mud, laying adobes and putting strange solar objects on our roof. Suspending judgment, we found, went a long way, and the tolerant attitude allowed us to fit into the North Valley community even though we were newcomers. And there were always solutions. Mark bought the pigs—with the exception of the Vietnamese pot-bellied one who could do tricks—and our neighbor shipped them off to a relative for a matanza. Our neighbors were happy. So were those to whom we gave the pigs.

Celia is long gone, but 45 years later we still see those tortilla windows in our back yard every day. They remind me that tolerance has been one of the key attributes of the North Valley.

5

A Rough Draft

1975-1979

"Do you think they get *The New York Times* there?" I
asked my husband, Mark, as we drove through Tijeras
canyon and into Albuquerque in 1975. Until then, it had not
crossed my mind that I might be cut off from the events
of Washington, D.C., the business news, and my favorite
columnists. The very thought frightened me. I had anchored
my day with newspapers. My father, a newspaperman,
brought home *The Philadelphia Evening Bulletin, The
Washington Post,* and sometimes *The Philadelphia Inquirer*
every afternoon. The high school history classes I taught
started with current events. I had seen how photojournalism
and TV footage could end a war, expose lies, and affect
elections. I was in awe of investigative journalism and I
gobbled up long articles with facts that journalists fit together
to provide evidence that would bring even presidents to

justice. Like so many Americans, I had adopted intrepid *Post* reporters Bob Woodward and Carl Bernstein as my heroes.

What would I do without access to my daily news sources? Mark wasn't too worried. He had his architecture program at UNM to occupy his time and energy. But until I could find a fix for my news habit, and something constructive to do, I was at a loss.

~

It caught my eye immediately amidst the scraps of paper tacked over one another, the advertisements for blood donations, houses for rent, and something called Eckankar. "Volunteers needed for alternative newspaper," it announced. I got my ice cream from the counter of the deserted café, called the Hippo, and then returned to the bulletin board. The ad offered the opportunity to write, to take photos, and join a group effort to produce a bi-weekly tabloid, a copy of which was right there in an adjoining rack.

The cover had a high contrast photo of a sheriff from someplace called Rio Arriba standing with his arms crossed in the middle of the street. The headline read "The Black Gloves of Balthazar." I started leafing through the paper. There were articles on hippies in Placitas, UNM's new women's studies program, and other local stuff. It seemed to be covering an entirely different world than the daily paper, the *Albuquerque Journal.* Here were articles about uranium mining (of which I knew nothing), political marches (I had seen none of these in New Mexico), problems with Governor Jerry Apodaca (who was he?), and someplace called the South Valley.

I figured I might as well give *Seers Catalog,* as the tabloid was called, a ring.

My first assignment sent me to Albuquerque's South Valley (ah, there it was, just nearby) to cover what I later found out was a continuing saga of water pollution from farm operations. There had been a rumor of a "blue baby" born nearby. Blue babies, I found out, had skin shaded blue from reduced blood oxygen levels because of nitrates from farm operations in the local drinking water.

I interviewed the owners of Schwartzman's feedlot where the cows were packed so close together they emitted a sort of steam. On the tour they conducted, the stench made my eyes tear and my stomach heave. I fidgeted for a Kleenex in my purse. The owners vigorously denied any connection, but the proximity, the smell, and the water used to hose down the cows was leaching into the ground before my eyes. Years later, when I sat on the New Mexico Senate's Conservation Committee, I realized that groundwater contamination from dairy operations was a major environmental issue, requiring lining of pits and limitations on density. But then I knew nothing of this. Only rumors of the blue baby.

They put my article on the second page of the paper, along with the photo I had ineptly snapped. Wow. I was hooked. My work was in print, prominently displayed, on the first try. Underlings at *The Philadelphia Evening Bulletin,* where I had worked in 1968 on the women's page (I corrected spelling errors in wedding announcements from the elite Main Line families), waited years for this and now here I was, a stranger in town, almost on the front page.

In pursuing the feedlot story, I had stumbled upon a gold mine—the Southwest Research and Information Center, then on Harvard Avenue. It was founded by Peter and Katherine Montague, both alumni of early consumer protection guru Ralph Nader's original group, Nader's Raiders. Nader's best-selling book *Unsafe at Any Speed* had spurred changes in the auto industry, and Peter and Katherine were dedicated to using research to extend reform into other areas. Both were slim, attractive, and educated, and they had abandoned the East Coast to come west. Soon enough, they became my heroes, crusaders for the environment, for the victims of mining and the inhabitants of what they called a "national sacrifice area." I never met two people so driven and so passionate. I often found myself in the small, disheveled office stuffed with environmental impact statements, transcripts of committee hearings, and obscure reports on uranium tailings, superfund sites, and nuclear waste.

Here were *The New York Times* newspapers I had wondered about—in piles and stacks, in milk crates, in closets, and back rooms. I can still smell that dusty paperwork, hear the filing cabinets opening and closing, and remember the passionate arguments, the anger about water contamination, about political inaction, or outright collusion with extractive industries. I still hear them in my head and I still pay heed.

Every two weeks the back of my yellow 1973 Subaru station wagon was full to the roof with bundles of *Seers* tabloids bound for scores of newsstands, restaurants, head shops, and car repair places around town. It was my job (along with everything else) to deliver them and sell ads for the next issue as I dropped in on retailers and restaurant owners like Bea and Jake of the Sanitary Tortilla Factory at 2nd and Lead. They were good for at least a half hour conversation and often a free Mexican lunch.

I got to interview land grant activist Reyes Lopez Tijerina, comedian Dick Gregory, and Muhammad Ali as they jogged cross country to bring attention to hunger, stopping in Socorro. I wrote long-form journalistic pieces about the Westland

Development Corporation (the former Atrisco Land Grant) and the National College of Business (a fly-by night private college which was scamming veterans) and the first women admitted to the New Mexico Military Institute. My comrades wrote about the AMREP Corporation and early real estate swindles on the West Side of Albuquerque and corruption among elected officials (imagine that!). We got letters to the editor from a curiously literate prisoner in Arizona—Jimmy Santiago Baca, who later became a popular New Mexico poet. I would pick up cartoons of fat cats smoking cigars and crushing lowly workers under their jackboots drawn by novelist John Nichols, the author of *The Milagro Beanfield War.* He would send the illustrations down from Taos by bus to the Greyhound station.

At the paper, we talked about how we offered an alternative to the mainstream and asked if there was such a thing as objective journalism. We covered women, Native Americans, and Chicanos as newsmakers and used them as sources, not afterthoughts. We asked the hard questions, investigated, traced the power dynamics, and cast blame when it was clear. We tried to be a thorn in the side of the daily papers, but occasionally we cooperated with the *Albuquerque Journal* and *The Arizona Republic* to research stories about land swindles and organized crime in the Southwest. In the aftermath of the assassination of *Arizona Republic* reporter Don Bolles in 1976, investigative reporters and editors from around the country worked together in a formal syndicate to expose corruption—a kind of journalistic cooperation that is rare today. We didn't know it then, but we were living in the afterglow of the 1973 Watergate scandal that forced the resignation of President Richard Nixon and ushered in a new golden age of activist journalism. Investigative reporters spurred changes and brought down presidents.

Each issue was a crisis. The stakes for every story were high. Police brutality was breaking the back of La Raza Unida in Rio Arriba County, Navajo miners had built their homes with uranium tailings in the Northwest part of the state, and the Department of Energy was planning a nuclear waste disposal facility near Carlsbad.

The night before the paper was due at the printer, united in purpose and determination, we would stay up all night, laying out the paper in a small house off San Isidro Street, in the heart of what I knew later as Senate District 13. The "after parties" featured music by Bob Dylan, Carlos Santana, and a cast of characters unlike any I had known back East. Our gang was intergenerational, hip, radical, funny, driven, and Chicano, with connections to Pine Ridge, the Weather Underground, and the *Monkey Wrench Gang*. We had become a collective, where credit, poverty, tortillas, beer, cigarettes, and concert tickets were all shared.

Every one of us knew how to wield the X-ACTO blade, crop photos, lay out the calendar, typeset the classifieds, use a light table, fashion a lede paragraph, negotiate an ad contract, quote sources accurately, and write headlines that grabbed attention. There were no formal positions at the paper. Even the editorship rotated. No one had training as a journalist.

By 1976 we had moved to a real office—a converted white rectangle on Coal Avenue, which smelled like burned torti-llas, musty newspapers, and sour dirty dishes. The furniture was all donated. Broken newspaper racks were thrown in the corners and we were periodically robbed. But the hunger for change, the ambition of youth, and the sense that we were on the front lines, kept us going until some of us finally got tired of food stamps, burned out, and sought regular employment. *Seers* finally folded in 1978, but by then it had become one of the longer lasting of the slew of alternative newspapers to spring up around the country in the afterglow of the 1960s.

It was just what I had been seeking. For this stranger in New Mexico, with no cultural ties and no family outside of my husband, *Seers* provided a point of connection to this exciting new place, a source of tough new projects and most important, a community.

I used to joke that *Seers* gave me an excuse to stick my nose into other peoples' business, find out what was happening, and then try to make something useful come out of it. But it was no joke. I didn't know it then, but it was the start of something bigger, which ultimately led me to the New Mexico Senate.

~

I continued to write, freelancing for various newspapers and magazines, throughout the 1980s. The topics were often the ones I started covering at *Seers*—uranium mining, the Waste Isolation Pilot Plant (WIPP), women, and environmental activism. For a while I was a stringer for the *Navajo Times,* covering urban Indian issues in Albuquerque and putting my copy on the bus to Gallup where Bill Donovan, then the editor, picked it up. I was paid five cents per column inch.

In 1979, I was thrilled to get a byline in *The New York Times* for a story about Bokum Resources, a local uranium company which was poised to supply the proposed Shoreham Nuclear Plant in Long Island. Trouble was, the ore was to be milled near Marquez, NM, in a mill built in the middle of an arroyo, which periodically drained to the Rio Puerco. It wasn't a problem for the New Mexico Environment Department, which was going to issue a permit until the press (including me) started asking questions. It seemed that Mr. Bokum was a friend of then Governor Jerry Apodaca and his partner in a local racquetball club. In the end, an anti-nuke group out of Placitas called the Sandoval Environmental Action Committee, along with several Rio Grande pueblos and opponents of Shoreham in New York, thwarted the deal.

The rare victory was sweet. It fueled my faith that aggressive, accurate newspaper coverage could make change.

And so I continued with a major investigation into the Los Alamos Scientific Laboratory (now Los Alamos National Laboratory), where the atomic bomb was born. My partner was Phil Niklaus, an environmental reporter who had just quit the *Albuquerque Journal.* One of the photos for the piece was of steel drums ready for disposal.

They looked like ordinary 55-gallon drums, a little taller maybe, with thick lids like the kind you might use to cover your takeout soup. They were standing in an uncovered, wide ditch on the mesa.

The young reporters, Phil and I, asked the scientists how secure the drums were, and if there was any contamination of the surrounding area. It was 1979, the year of Three Mile Island. The basic message of most of the Los Alamos engineers that year, as we investigated radiation and waste disposal practices, was this:

Experts agree, everything is fine.

It wasn't enough for us, for the Center for Investigative Journalism, or in the end, for the *Albuquerque Journal,* which published our work as an eight-part, front-page series, "How

Safe is New Mexico's Atomic City?" We spent months combing through technical documents in the Lab's library: environmental surveillance reports, accident and cancer rates, and other historic documents. Meanwhile, news of Karen Silkwood, the Kerr-McGee Chemical Corporation, and that year's huge anti-nuclear March on Washington came and went in *The New York Times.* It became the stuff of movies.

Our research came to an abrupt end when the Lab closed the library to the public, i.e., us. But it was too late—we had read all the reports, learned the history, and were already interviewing the keepers of the secrets, the defenders against the siege.

They each had a story. Dr. George Voelz had one. It was about how the elevated breast cancer rates in Los Alamos County were due to socioeconomic factors, not radiation. Harold Agnew, director of the Lab, chalked up the higher rates of intestinal cancer to green chile and rich foods. The best antidote to tritium contamination (a radionuclide escaping from buried waste into the atmosphere) was to drink lots of beer, another said. It was true that plutonium from the old days, when the first atomic bombs were made, was dumped into the nearby canyons. And yes, it was periodically carried to the Rio Grande by snowmelt and run off. But not to worry, said Dr. Lamar Johnson, the levels were insignificant and less than background radiation.

We took notes. We documented. We drove back from Los Alamos through the Jemez Mountains, shaking our heads, wondering about the phenomenon called "denial." George Voelz's wife, we found out, had breast cancer. More accidents came to light. And now, 40 years later, those 55-gallon drums we had seen, the ones with the lids, have come back to bite the Lab.

Who knows how many were transported to the WIPP site in southern New Mexico before the big accident? Even the special bypass built around Santa Fe for them, and the widened roads in eastern New Mexico, couldn't prevent the inevitable. A few years ago, the whole WIPP site closed down for two years, after an explosion and fire involving one of those drums. It had been packed in a substance akin to kitty litter. They didn't use kitty litter in 1979, when we did our story. But I'm sure they would have told us it was more than adequate.

~

In the following years, I continued to freelance, learning about New Mexico's chronic poverty, its history of resource exploitation, and the struggles of Hispanics and Native Americans to retain their land and identity. I spoke with statistics, painted a scene, quoted specialists, and led people to their own conclusions about the dangers of plutonium or nitrates in the groundwater. My notes and clippings formed a rough draft of the history of New Mexico in the 70s and early 80s. I knew how to ask all the questions and describe the problem. I knew the victims and the executioners, and I could cast blame on government or one special interest group or another. What I gradually realized was that I needed to search for solutions, not just report the problems.

Inevitably that realization led to politics.

Long ago I had concluded that politics was the way resources were distributed and used. Every decision about that was based on values, namely whether the leaders believed that everyone should get an equal shot, no matter their race, creed, or sex. Solutions to the problems I had described could come mostly from mayors, governors, city councilors, legislators, senators, and congresspeople. It was then that I realized that it was time to put down the pen and pick up the paddle.

6

Picking Up the Paddle

Election Night, November 1988

Tom Udall pushed on the side door leading to the parking lot of the Albuquerque Marriott, but it would not budge. It was too heavy. The EXIT sign glared red, but there would be no exit. The chilly November night would not become the respite he so desperately needed.

Tom turned and looked back at the crowd of reporters reluctantly pursuing him down the hotel corridor and smiled for the cameras one last time. It was the last thing he wanted to do.

Charlie, who had covered the campaign from the start, was as embarrassed as all the rest. He yelled a final question, something about Tom's concession speech in the 1988 congressional race. Had it been premature? Weren't there votes still to be counted?

Earlier, the ballroom had been jammed with local candidates, campaign workers, tribal officials in from the reservation, and hangers-on of all stripes. They had guzzled all the free booze that the now-closed bar had to offer and ravaged the buffet table down to the condiments. Those were gone too. Only empty saucers of mustard and salsa remained.

All of us on the campaign had streamed in from "the field"—from polling places around town, last-minute phone banks, some from the County Clerk's office, and one from a TV station where results had been tabulated early. We picked up yard signs as we went—from yards, from intersections, from storefronts—and threw them into the backs of our cars. Tomorrow they would be trash.

We had set up the computers, precinct maps, and a huge tally sheet in the small hotel room reserved for the staff. It was on the third floor, away from the madding crowd. The bathtub was iced with beer. The omnipresent coffee machine, brought in from the headquarters, miraculously was still working, dispensing its foul necessity. The candidate's wife, Jill, sat in the corner speaking to no one. She looked up when Tom opened the door, a sheaf of computer printouts in his hand.

He had come to thank the staff, to say how brilliant we had been, how we had been creative in targeting just the right voters with just the right message. We had been agile, he said, resourceful in our response to those dark TV ads with the dreaded voice, the avalanche of false mailers saying he hadn't paid off his student loans and wasn't from here, anyway.

The TV, long muted, began to flash images from the ten o'clock news. KOAT was live, carrying Tom's opponent, Steve Schiff, giving his victory speech before throngs of cheering supporters at the Hilton downtown.

"Yes, we fell a little short," he told us. But the campaign would live on. He lied. Our innovative techniques—the way we used data—would set the standard for the politics of the future. And the friends we had made here would be friends forever.

The young press secretary, who had been so tough, so strategic, silently began to cry. Only I knew because that young press secretary was me.

"Look around you—and you will see the leaders of the future—chiefs of staff, cabinet secretaries, and even senators," Tom said.

"Your day will come quickly. It may not be tonight, but it will come soon. And I will always be your friend, there to cheer you on and support you, as you have done for me."

"And now," he said with a fake smile, "can someone get me one of those beers?"

~

I could tell you details like that about each political campaign I worked on in the decade spanning 1984-1994. The clunky computer, one of the first used in a campaign, sitting in Judy Pratt's storefront office in the South Valley in 1984; Brant Calkin's flat top and his knowledge of all things environmental; Pat Baca's inflammatory concession speech in 1989.

Serving as a press secretary for Democratic candidates was a logical extension of my freelance journalism career. I knew the players from interviews I had done, or articles I had written. So, when Judy Pratt, a representative from the University District, asked me if I could write a few press releases, maybe craft a few speeches and talking points for her insurgent campaign for the US Senate in 1984, I was game. She was, after all, one of the first women to run for a statewide office, other than secretary of state, a post traditionally held by women.

Soon it became much more than media relations. Campaigns have a way of eating everything in their path. Personalities become larger than life. The decisions are agonizing, the conflicts magnified, and the pace grueling. Things have to happen. Your heart is beating. You can't say no.

I can date every year of my life during that period by the political campaign I was working on and the people I encountered—the diehard environmentalists on Brandt Calkin's campaign for land commissioner, the women with babies on Judy's campaign for the US Senate, and the Democratic regulars I met campaigning for Tom Udall and Pat Baca. For my crowd, campaigns were where we met our friends, decided what to do with our lives, where to put our kids in day care, whether to go to graduate school, or move to another part of town. They were where we formed a support system—a network—long before the word became trendy.

In July 1984 I didn't go to the Democratic Convention with the rest of the women on Judy Pratt's campaign. I watched from my living room with my two-year old daughter Abby. I was frustrated to miss the historic convention when the first woman, Geraldine Ferraro, was nominated for vice president. I listened to New York Governor Mario Cuomo and Civil Rights Activist Rev. Jesse Jackson, who both gave keynote addresses. I took notes, got ideas for the speeches I would write, and tended the campaign headquarters in the South Valley.

I was busy writing press releases on my new Selectric typewriter, getting them xeroxed at the nearby copy shop, delivering them in person to the newsrooms of the *Albuquerque Journal* and the *Albuquerque Tribune,* then co-located downtown in a brick building at 7th and Silver. I rose early to call rural radio stations during AM drive time. I'd attach an alligator clip to the handset of my landline, with a cord running to my tape recorder, which I'd have cued up with statements from Judy on various topics. I'd press the button and transmit. These were the days when radio stations actually had local news, not just national feeds, and it was amazing how much of our stuff was picked up.

I was a do-it-yourself news transmitter long before social media made it easy. Soon I acquired a photocopy machine of my own, and then, miracle of miracles, a fax machine. By the mid-80s I got one of the first Macintosh computers and fashioned a few basic newsletters and brochures. I was ready for the revolution and I was the Minister of Propaganda.

Judy Pratt's campaign was not my first.

My daughter's pediatrician, Dr. Sue Brown, had drafted me the year before, literally as I lay on the delivery room table, to serve as campaign manager in her bid for the Albuquerque School Board. How could I refuse? She knew I had a new baby—she was holding her in her arms. I'd be home anyway, she said. "It's the perfect time to make phone calls." Her smile assured me there would be no guilt involved.

Even that was not my first campaign. Long before I got to New Mexico, I worked for a "peace candidate" running for Congress in Beltsville, Maryland, in 1966.

He happened to be a Republican. That didn't matter. He was anti-war and a good guy, an accountant. I can still remember driving his old Rambler with a huge box built onto the roof to display a four-sided sign proclaiming "Bill Martin for Congress!" It hung over the sides of the car, and it creaked and rattled as I drove along the beltway, into suburban shopping centers and busy intersections. It was clearly—and dangerously—homemade. How did I wind up in Prince George's County with this particular candidate? I had met him at a demonstration in D.C., on the steps of the capitol or at the Washington Monument during one of the huge mobilizations against the war in Vietnam. Or maybe it was some Quaker connection? I can't remember. Anyway, he put me up in his basement where I was stationed at a card table, covered with index cards upon which his wife had written addresses and phone numbers, straight out of the phone book. When I was not out with him at events (which often featured the "reform" candidate for governor, Spiro Agnew, who later became Nixon's vice president), I was in the basement, looking up more phone numbers, and making endless calls to voters, just like I did in the time of coronavirus for the 2020 election. I think I was the campaign's only volunteer.

~

Campaign technology had taken a step up after the mid-80s, but not by much. The Brant Calkin campaign was a barebones affair, with little money, but lots of enterprise and moxie—all emanating from the office of the NM Sierra Club on San Pedro Drive, located directly across from the state fairgrounds. Brant had been the national president of the Sierra Club and now he was running for state land commissioner. (I know, state land commissioner? Half of my time was spent explaining what the uniquely Western office did.) He was a scientist. He knew what cattle ranching could do to streambeds, why endangered species were important, and who was who in the Bureau of Land Management. I was in awe of his knowledge of the Southwest.

The Calkin campaign was where I learned about the *Monkey Wrench Gang,* who John Wesley Powell was, why the cattle growers were a powerful force in New Mexico, and how the spotted owl and the willow flycatcher were not trivial. It was a campaign of environmentalists who rafted the Taos Box on the Rio Grande, hiked into San Pedro Parks Wilderness on the weekends, and did service projects clearing trails with the Sierra Club in the Grand Canyon. I had run into some of these folks writing articles on groundwater or uranium issues, but it was only then that I realized the growing strength of the local environmental movement. Here were savvy activists with mailing lists that included thousands, a nationwide network, a phone tree, and a messianic zeal.

I didn't know it then, but they would become my allies, working with me in the halls of the legislature, and campaigning in the North Valley to protect the river and the bosque for the next three decades.

The environmental movement had been growing since the mid-70s when I first encountered it at the Southwest Research and Information Center. In New Mexico it was intertwined with Native communities and Hispanic land grants, all victims of resource exploitation and environmental injustice. As opposed to California, New Mexico's most dedicated activists were not older, well-heeled liberals who wanted to preserve wild places. They were radical young people like I had become. We asked whether a pollutant exceeded the standard, knew about the carcinogens, and radioactive waste. We saw the connection between various types of exploitation and knew that political change was the only hope.

Lynda Taylor, with her Boston accent and boundless energy was, among other things, the volunteer coordinator. She had participated in thousands of community struggles on the reservation and against the Waste Isolation Pilot Plant, and she later prowled the halls of the legislature. Early on she had organized environmental voters into the Conservation Voters Alliance, published a scorecard for legislators, pushed the Environment Department for stricter groundwater contamination rules. Like so many of the activists I knew then, Lynda was a zealot. Listening to her spout out facts, national connections, history, requests, demands, and things to do was exhausting. But she made things happen. Lynda had a twinkle in her eye and nerves of steel. You could sense the adrenaline and feel the intensity. It was best not to get too close.

But I did get close. I couldn't help it. I went above and beyond my role as media person. I draped banners from bridges over the freeway with other staff on election morning. It was a cheap stunt to gain "visibility" without spending any money—one of the first in Albuquerque. It worked. The TV cameras were there. It reminded me of the 1960s.

The people power almost propelled Brant to victory, but a snowstorm in northern New Mexico on election day discouraged voter turnout in San Miguel and Mora counties. Brant lost by a whisker to Bill Humphries, a conservative rancher who was funded by the office's traditional constituents—the ranchers and oil and gas interests who held leases on state land.

In spite of the loss, I was encouraged by what a small bank of organized, intelligent activists could do without money or much party support. Brant got 49.6% of the vote in a year when Republicans swept every statewide office. He pulled no punches. He minced no words in his support for wilderness, conservation, and strict environmental control. In those days before state campaigns became referendums on national wedge issues, ordinary people were receptive to his folksy approach. New Mexicans, it seemed, valued their mountains, their rivers, their elk, their fish, and most of all their land. They wanted to protect their special places—a lesson I took with me into the New Mexico Senate.

~

Finally, this time I thought I was on the winning side. Tom Udall had won a heavily contested primary for the congressional seat left open by the unexpected retirement of Manuel Lujan in 1988. He now faced Republican District Attorney Steve Schiff. The environmentalists, the progressives, we all flocked to the campaign, attracted by the Udall legacy, the possibilities presented by an open seat and the end of the Reagan era.

The storefront office on Central in the Nob Hill area was always full. Desks were arranged classroom style, in orderly rows facing Central Avenue. The Central Deli was next door and Barry Soprano often sent trays of bagels or tuna salad sandwiches. Canvassers fresh from the Calkin campaign came and went. They knew where to go, what precincts were swing, and which were safe.

There was an office manager, volunteer coordinators, fundraisers, phone bank coordinators, family members—all in one large room. Celebrities would come by—people Tom's father Stewart Udall knew from the Kennedy administration. Robert Redford did an event. Real money was raised. The Democratic Congressional Campaign Committee dispatched a media buyer from out of town. The national party often told us what to do but we often disagreed.

By that time, I had acquired a fax machine and a Macintosh computer. I was ready to roll out the releases, the poll results, the list of endorsers, and the position papers. My press list expanded. I tried to think of ways to get Tom into unexpected media slots—the early morning news (i.e., 5 a.m.), the sports section (he was a marathon runner) or the food page (he was a whole foods nut and nary a piece of junk food crossed his lips).

Tom Udall did not suffer from a lack of coverage. His appeal was not all my doing. He was part of a legendary Southwestern family. His father was an Interior Secretary under President John F. Kennedy; his uncle Mo a beloved congressman from Arizona. He had national support. Contributions came in from around the country, even before the internet made it easy. He was good looking, pleasant, and he later became a powerful force in New Mexico politics. In 1988, however, his opponents painted him as an outsider, a pretty boy, a lightweight coasting on his family connections. In the last days of the campaign Tom was hit with a fierce negative campaign, based on a claim about him not paying his student loans. It was the year that negative campaigns kicked off in earnest, with Republican consultant Lee Atwater rolling out scary images. The best known was that of Willie Horton, a black man who had escaped a Massachusetts prison while on a weekend furlough, raped a white woman, and stabbed her husband. Atwater—and the George H. Bush campaign—blamed Gov. Michael Dukakis, the Democratic candidate. Tom was philosophic about the last-minute attack on him, and our own frantic attempts to counter it.

"A lie has traveled around the world twice by the time the truth has pulled on its boots," he said, quoting Mark Twain via Mo Udall, his wise, humorous uncle.

Dukakis lost in a landslide that year, and Tom lost by a few thousand votes. I was devastated. All our work. All the people who had come together as a family. All the early morning breakfasts before setting out clipboard in hand; all the volunteers who had traveled from so far.

The day after, it was torture arranging the follow-up interviews, taking down the signs. I saved one in my garage for years, adding it to the collection now hanging from the rafters. All my candidates had lost. Sure, I was building skills—writing speeches, holding news conferences, and learning how to frame the issues to persuade the public. Unwittingly, I had built a little public relations business. In the next few years my clients would include banks and hospitals. I could charge a higher fee to the big clients, a lower one to the non-profits whose causes I believed in, and to the candidates on whom I would not give up.

But there was no denying it. All my candidates had lost (except for Dr. Sue Brown, my pediatrician, who won her school board race handily, having delivered most of the babies in the South Valley). I felt terrible. I commiserated with others from the various campaigns. We did not give up, but it was hard times. It was the 1980s.

Gradually I realized that I was not the loser, and, actually losing is sometimes just the beginning. I was accumulating allies from different parts of the community—environmentalists, women, Democratic regulars at the precinct level, teachers, and labor activists. I didn't see it that way at the time, but I do now.

Over the next years we continued to help one another, bound together by the losses we had sustained, and our determination to make a difference, to change things for the better. We grew together. Some of us (like me) would later work on our issues from the inside. Others would become professional organizers or start non-profits, agricultural co-ops, and think tanks.

In 1995 I would run my own campaign for the Albuquerque City Council, losing once again (by nine votes this time), but laying the foundation for another campaign, which I would win overwhelmingly the following year.

The political alliances I was building during the 1980s shifted in the next few years, but most of us did not give up on politics. We persisted. There would be no walking away from the issues of economic inequality and historic injustice that we had discovered. We were building a progressive community. This was a permanent campaign.

~

A few months later, Tom Udall called his former staffers together in the backyard of his former campaign manager Arturo Sandoval's house on 15th Street. He was starting over. He wanted to ask us if he should run again—for Congress or attorney general? He said $250,000 in TV advertisements and in name recognition was a terrible thing to waste. At the time, I was tired of failure—tired of losing—and was not much use. He decided on the attorney general option, ran, and won in 1990, serving until 1999 when he became the US Congressman from the northern district. In 2008 he was elected to the US Senate, from which he retired in 2020.

Tom became one of my most valuable allies in my years in the New Mexico Senate. We partnered on reducing the price of prescription drugs and campaign finance reform, both easy issues to talk about on the campaign trail, but almost insurmountable once on the inside.

He remains my hero.

7

The Ward Heeler and the Woman

1987

THE COFFIN TRAVELED SLOWLY UP THE AISLE of Old Town's San Felipe de Neri church, past the church regulars, the guys from the Monte Carlo restaurant, a few party officials, and family scattered among the pews. The huge maple box was born by sturdy young men in gray work shirts, blue jeans, or navy pants. I thought they were the uniforms of the Solid Waste Department at first. It was one of the last places that Tom Castillo, North Valley Ward Chair, matanza organizer, and political aide worked. I was touched by the loyalty of Albuquerque city employees. My mind went to TV broadcasts I'd seen of funerals in New York City where police patrols escorted the hearse down Fifth Avenue and hundreds of uniformed officers formed a sea of blue surrounding the bereaved family.

Later, at the reception in Duranes, I found out from Tom's sister, that no, the Castillos were all Dallas Cowboys fans, and the pallbearers were Tom's nephews, sporting the colors.

Tom and I were tangled up in the grassroots of North Valley politics for at least two decades, sometimes opponents, more often allies, and in the end becoming old friends. Born and bred in Old Town, Tom knew all the politicians and had helped half of them get elected. He served as an aide to my predecessor in the New Mexico Senate, Senator Tito Chavez, and was one of Mayor Martin Chavez's go-to guys. He'd worked in almost every state and city department.

He knew how to dig the hole at the mantanza and make sure the *chicharrones* were crispy. He had a connection with the golf pros for fundraisers and could get a good pig from Valencia County. Tom was low-key, the picture of polyester practicality, with his crop of black hair always the same. His constant companions Sam Garcia and Spider attracted attention. Tom could melt undetected into his native habitat.

I was the newbie in the North Valley, just off the boat. True, by the time I met Tom I had lived on Meadow View Drive for over 15 years and campaigns were part of my story, too. I had been the communications director for Rep. Judy Pratt, the first woman to run for the US Senate in New Mexico. And I worked for Tom Udall when he ran for Manuel Lujan's congressional seat in 1988. But for Tom Castillo, and most of the politicos who stood guard over the rusty local Democratic machine, I was an outsider.

It was a view I would have to contend with throughout my political career. I was a woman, an outsider, and an Anglo, for God's sake—three definite strikes against me. In the North Valley, a heavily Democratic area, the entire legislative delegation had been composed of Hispanic males for as long as anyone could remember. And once in office, these guys tended to stay there forever, since there are no term limits for the legislature or the city council in New Mexico. Primary challengers were few and far between. And the party machine was falling into disuse, with fewer and fewer attendees at ward and precinct meetings.

I had to beg for information on the location of my ward meeting back in 1984, and once I found it, I was greeted by a disorganized mess. No one wanted to be a precinct official or knew how to canvass their neighborhood.

Meanwhile, on a national scale, Ronald Reagan was cracking down on "welfare queens" and building up the military, and George Bush Senior was sending us all off in search of "a thousand points of light" to seek out private solutions to public problems. A conservative Cowboy Coalition had captured the New Mexico House of Representatives and begun fighting Governor Toney Anaya. But there was a progressive uprising afoot, and I was part of it.

Pam Minzner, Anne Bingaman, and a troop of crusaders for women's rights had persuaded the New Mexico Legislature to ratify the Equal Rights Amendment, giving hope to women, who slowly began to run for office. The Women's Political Caucus helped provide training and information on issues like pay equity, abortion rights, and credit reform. The women supported each other and found the courage to ask for contributions, to stand up for themselves and not just lick envelopes. We started at the bottom—getting appointed to boards and commissions, running for the school board, and even running for ward chair.

The women joined forces in local campaigns with environmentalists, teachers, students, and a few stray labor organizers. They formed a new group of progressives who saw a vacuum at ground level and worked to find and train candidates to fill it. The NM Progressive Political Action Committee (ProPAC) tackled the Cowboy Coalition in the legislature with gusto and talked politics incessantly. We saw our enemies as the boring, same-old-stuff politicians who, even though they were Democrats, never questioned the political grip of oil and gas or land developers. We attended union conventions and got elected to seemingly meaningless positions—all with the aim of starting real reform. Future Minnesota Senator Paul Wellstone, who was credited years later for reigniting a progressive movement, would have been proud.

~

So it was that I found myself in a small room, the ceramics room actually, of the Duranes Community Center as the line for the ward meeting extended outside the building on a chilly March evening in 1987. In keeping with my newfound political activism, I had been calling around. I decided that if I got enough of my ProPAC friends, women, anti-bridge activists, and pals from the neighboring precincts to show up, I could be ward chair. From there I could support the local campaigns of my progressive buddies and have influence on who was the county chair or the nominee for governor.

Years later, I replay the meeting over and over in my mind.

The line was moving steadily. There were young people who had responded to my call, often with children at their heels, with voter registration cards in hand, as I had instructed. Some had "Stop the Bridge" stickers or buttons for Democratic candidates in the upcoming primary. They were there to vote for their ally on the Montaño bridge issue, then coming to a head. I was heartened by the arrivals—there was Abe from the food co-op, Dr. Guinn from the First Choice Health Clinic, a group of teachers from the Montessori school, Roy Chavira, the postman, Gabe Chavez, and a few other neighbors from Meadow View Drive. And there, God bless him, was Joe Ramirez, probably one of the only party regulars to support me. He had brought his wife and daughter.

Just then I was called over to the registration desk by a young volunteer I had asked to help with registration.

"This just doesn't look right," the teenager said. "There are sixteen voters registered at this one address—and they all registered last week."

"But do they actually live there?" I asked, recognizing a few of the names.

"Doesn't matter," said another registrar sitting at the desk. "Sometimes the children want to keep voting at the same place they've always voted so they keep their registration at their old address."

"Yeah, but how can anyone have sixteen children?" the teenager asked, as one of the other registrars called over my opponent and the current ward chair, Tom Castillo.

"This is perfectly legal. We've been doing it this way for years," he said. "Let them in."

"Okay, but I am filing a complaint with the credentials committee," said the disgruntled teenager.

"Not to worry," I whispered, "I've been keeping count. With the ten other supporters in line, I think we've got it covered."

But I spoke too soon. The ward heeler had yet to weigh in.

Most of Tom's folks, the regulars, had arrived early, well before the 7 p.m. deadline when registration closed, but just before seven o'clock, a gang of scraggly street people I didn't recognize began to stream in. Some said they were registered voters and, as others waited, they argued with the registrars who said they were not on the list and probably lived in another ward. Others didn't care and just spilled into the room, bringing with them a faint smell of alcohol. The noise level rose.

I went over to Tom and said, "You can't be serious, can you? This is ridiculous. These people aren't registered in our ward. This is something out of the handbook marked crooked."

"Don't worry, they won't be voting," said Tom. "They just came to support me. Not everybody who lives here is a yuppie, you know. They're part of our community, too, and they just want to be part of the process, even though they can't vote. I'll leave it to you and all these new Democrats you recruited to register them later."

His look said he had been through it all before with new people who showed up at meetings but never did any of the door-to-door grunt work.

Among the seedy group, I recognized Dave Duran, a local fixture who had once been a neighborhood leader but who was now reduced to life on the streets. The thrill of Dave's life was standing outside the Duranes polling place on election day with a sign for his favorite candidate. There was no denying the fact that these were actually my neighbors. Tom was right about that.

Finally, at 7:15 the meeting was called to order by the ward chair, Tom Castillo, who much to everyone's surprise, turned the meeting over to the vice chair, who acted as temporary chairman.

"I'm running for office here, so I don't think it's proper to run the meeting," he said.

After a report from the credentials committee confirmed that there were 114 people at the meeting, nominations for the office of ward chair were officially opened.

I had persuaded a friend to nominate me, emphasizing my activism for causes that defined the Democratic Party—the environment, equal rights for women and minorities, and work for some of our best Democratic candidates. The old guard talked big, he said, but I had actually been the one knocking on doors and making the calls to get people out to vote. A number of heads nodded in approval.

But just as Sam Garcia was beginning to nominate Tom, Dave Duran stumbled to the front of the room, mumbling something about his old man and the Virgin of Guadalupe.

"He's a good man, Tom Castillo," Duran said. "He went to San Felipe de Neri. He's been around here almost as long as I have. Finished high school, too, and once he got me a job with the County Public Works Department. I had that job for a long time, too, before I got sick. And what they say about him, about all those times the garbage guys went only to certain neighborhoods, where they got a 'tip' for their services? It ain't true. They always came to Duranes—my street was always clean, and I didn't give no tip."

Dave began to ramble on about *perros* (dogs) in the neighborhood, noise from the freeway, that stupid Chevy-on-a-

Stick that they were calling public art, and about how we really didn't need a panda at the zoo.

People were laughing. Finally, Tom nodded, and Duran stumbled to the back of the room.

Voting was then opened and people began to stuff their yellow slips into the ballot box. Then, their services no longer required, participants began to leave the building as quickly as they could.

The registrars proceeded to count the votes. The yellow slips were placed in piles as representatives from the Feldman and Castillo camps observed, along with a dozen or so curious precinct people.

"*Ganamos! Ganamos!*" Spider yelled, rushing toward the doorway as the last ballots were tallied. "*Tenemos*—we got it!"

The result was—65 for Castillo and 58 for Feldman.

"Oh no," one of my disappointed young supporters gasped.

"Oh wow, really close," said another.

"You really gave him a run for his money," said one of Castillo's supporters, holding out his hand to me. "I hope you serve as the vice chair, then we can be united for the fall election, no?"

"Yes," said another, "vice chair, that's a really important position."

Just as the temporary chair was about to announce the results and continue with the rest of the nominations, my young volunteer at the registration desk started yelling.

"Stop! Stop everything. We have to vote again. This is an outrage—and you know it," he said, glaring at Tom. "Can't you people do the math? 65 and 58 don't add up.

"Damn it," he said, his anger blooming. "You stuffed the ballot box. There were only 114 people registered to cast ballots here and somehow there were 123 ballots. You should be ashamed of yourselves."

"Re-vote, re-vote," a few diehard supporters started chanting, but by that time there were only a handful of party faithful remaining.

Suddenly, grabbing the microphone as if nothing had happened, Tom Castillo simply said, "This meeting is adjourned."

~

In the months following the meeting, the news spread to Democratic insiders. Tom kept a low profile, doing next to nothing in the next election. Drinking coffee and talking politics was enough. I swallowed hard and just kept working for the candidates I supported—Tom Udall for Congress and then Pat Baca for mayor. The regulars got to know me. And then something funny happened. I got a call from county headquarters that Tom had been disqualified as a ward chair. Months ago, he'd been told that he could not hold political office because he was a state employee. He never told his vice chair, of course. Why bother? Ward politics didn't mean that much anyway. At least that's what he always told me— to console me for my loss, I suppose.

I had held my tongue after the ballot box incident. Lots of friends urged me to protest but it didn't seem worth pursuing. Why badmouth someone whose help you might need in the future? We lived in the same neighborhood.

But word had gotten around. The people who mattered in the party knew what happened and they knew how I reacted. And now I was the ward chair.

Tom was wrong, though, ward politics did matter. The personal connections, and the opportunities to share common values, to eat and laugh together right here in a place we all knew and loved, was worth more than I ever could have imagined.

Gradually Tom and I worked together. We discovered that we were on the same side, backed the same candidates, and believed the same things. I found out his brother was disabled and that he spent much of his time taking care of him, especially after his mother died. We made common cause there, too, since I'd been doing media relations for several non-profits in this field—The Association for Retarded Citizens (ARC) of New Mexico (now The Arc of New Mexico), and Adelante Development Corp. I tried to help get him services for his brother and to move him up on the developmental disabilities waiting list.

His employment with the city prevented him from supporting me publicly when I ran for the city council against an incumbent in 1995, but I knew he was there, helping in the background.

When I ran for the senate in 1996, Tom surprised me—he supported me in the primary against a Hispanic woman he had known for years. In the end it was Spider, Tom, Sam, and me waving signs out on the median at Rio Grande and I-40 on election day. Spider waved his large, dirty bandana in circles around his head, crying *"Oye! Oye! Oye!"* like a mariachi. Nearby, at Duranes Elementary School, Dave Duran was holding my sign and telling surprised Anglos to vote for me.

8

The Bitch and
Moan Party

October 1991

LONG BEFORE THE #METOO MOVEMENT we believed her.
The women I worked with in the trenches in the 1970s and
1980s, the sisters who nursed babies, made telephone calls
for candidates, pushed for the Equal Rights Amendment to
prevent discrimination on the basis of sex, who laughed and
cried with me, were, for once, speechless.

Anita Hill had been courageous, dignified, and credible.
The all-male Senate Judiciary Committee, led by Senator Joe
Biden, had been disgraceful. The law professor was stranded
alone, sitting there in her green double-breasted dress, unable to present corroborating evidence.

Transfixed, I had listened to the October hearings on
a portable radio placed on a picnic table near Battleship

Rock, a landmark in the Jemez Mountains. My vacation was interrupted by anger, and then tears as Clarence Thomas was confirmed for the Supreme Court.

Two weeks after the hearing, unable to focus, a number of us settled on a consolation prize. We called it a Bitch and Moan Party. About forty of the most politically active women I knew crowded into our studio, bearing comfort food—mashed potatoes, chicken soup, lots of chocolate, and plenty of white wine. We were reclaiming the word *bitch*—what men had long called uppity women like us beginning to claim our due in the board room, in the university, or anywhere outside the kitchen and the nursery. They are still using the word in that way—ask Rep. Alexandria Ocasio-Cortez (widely known just by her AOC initials). Earlier this year Florida Congressman Ted Yoho accosted the liberal—and much maligned—Congresswoman from New York City on the steps of the Capitol in front of the press. He called her a "fucking bitch." Her response on the floor later became a classic denunciation of male abuse throughout the decades.

We had begun earlier, long before the Bitch and Moan Party, in the late 1970s, working for equal pay, equal credit, and day care. Most of us had young children and were just entering the workforce in earnest. By the late '80s a small group of us had become skilled in helping each other run for office. Some of us were veterans of the Judy Pratt campaign. In 1984 Judy, a state legislator from the university area, was the first woman in New Mexico to run for the US Senate. Members of the Women's Political Caucus, the National Organization of Women (NOW), and the American Association of University Women streamed in and out of her campaign headquarters in the South Valley, licked envelopes, and gave money. Credibility was a problem. Raising money was a problem. These were the early days. We used Christmas card lists, Rolodexes, rich relatives, and an old girls' network then under construction. Soon Emily's List appeared on the scene to help.

We had seen setbacks. The ratification of the Equal Rights Amendment (ERA) had failed. The anti-feminist Phyllis Schafley and the growing right wing succeeded in blocking the amendment in the needed states. Judy Pratt lost in a landslide to Pete Domenici. But this, the treatment of Anita Hill, was an emotional setback. It would not be the last. We had no idea that it would repeat itself in lurid detail in 2018 when a latter-day Senate Judiciary Committee overruled the testimony of Dr. Christine Blasey Ford, who shared details of a shameful sexual assault attempted by Supreme Court justice nominee Brett Kavanaugh. Once again, the majority of the committee, scorned the woman who dared to come forward at the last minute. Now controlled by Republicans, the committee sided with Kavanaugh, who made an emotional plea that he was a victim of mob psychology, just like Clarence Thomas. Women shouted from the back of the committee room and were ejected. At the end of the day, the Senate confirmed both Thomas and Kavanaugh, buying the story that it was they who had been the victims. They now sit on the Supreme Court for life.

~

The 1991 Bitch and Moan Party was in full swing. We discussed the women who were then running for the US Senate. We asked whether having women on the Senate Judiciary Committee would have changed the tone, the questions asked by Arlen Specter, Alan Simpson, Joe Biden, or Howell Heflin.

There were speeches by wannabe candidates, pleas for contributions and volunteers, and words of encouragement from the women who already held office. Checks were written, pollsters discussed, commitments made, and campaign managers hired.

The bitches had swung into action, and unlike 1984, that first "Year of the Woman," when candidates like Geraldine Ferraro and Judy Pratt had been sacrificial lambs put up by a party that did not support them, this time we would be successful.

The next year, in 1992, four Democratic women were elected to the US Senate—Barbara Boxer, Diane Feinstein, Patty Murray, and Carol Moseley Braun. Twenty-four won congressional seats. In New Mexico, the number of women in the state senate doubled. Women began in earnest to run for state courts, building on the pioneering work of Mary Walters, Pam Minzner, Patricia Madrid, and Susan Conway. 1992 was again dubbed the "Year of the Woman." A year later Ruth Bader Ginsburg became the first Democratic woman to serve on the Supreme Court.

In 2018—in the midst of the chaos created by Donald Trump—a record number of women were elected to the US House (including New Mexicans Debra Haaland and Xochitl Torres Small) and to the NM House, where women became the majority of the Democratic caucus.

In spite of the progress, the bitching and moaning has not stopped. It has grown louder. Faced with a president who bragged during his campaign that he could grab "pussy" with impunity, hundreds of thousands of women marched the day after Donald Trump's inauguration in Washington. It was the largest single-day demonstration in the history of the country. The marchers were joined by hundreds of thousands more in small towns and big cities throughout the country in places as remote as Fort Sumner, and Deming, New Mexico. Ten thousand marched in the snow in Santa Fe, and the gathering of pink hats at the Albuquerque Civic Plaza was one of the largest in that landmark's history. Everyone I know remembers where they were that day—and how we pledged to resist, and vote in every election.

The numbers of women elected to school boards, legislatures, and local offices increased in the following year. Ruth Bader Ginsburg, the longtime champion of women's rights, continued to inspire young women juggling professional careers and children, just as she had done herself, even before the Bitch and Moan Party. By 2020 Ginsburg, then a Supreme Court justice for 27 years, had become a cultural icon. Movies had been made; T-shirts, socks, and masks with her new rap moniker, the "Notorious RBG," sold like hotcakes. People prayed for her health; she received a standing ovation at the Santa Fe opera, which she attended every summer. Then, 42 days before the 2020 election, she died of pancreatic cancer. An outpouring of grief from liberal women, the women whom Donald Trump called the "nasty women," lasted a whole month. It was compounded by the ruthless move by the Senate Republicans to allow Trump to immediately name a successor, which he did even before Ginsburg had been buried.

According to the polls of that week, with RBG's death coming so close to the election, voters wanted to hold off and let the next president decide. It was an approach that Senate Majority Leader Mitch McConnell had insisted upon when he held up the confirmation of Merrick Garland, whom President Obama had appointed, for over nine months, so that the next president (Trump) could appoint his choice.

To make matters worse for women, Trump's conservative nominee, Amy Coney Barrett, is opposed to Roe v. Wade and will likely get a chance to overturn it on the high court. It is the last bastion before reproductive rights are left to the states to decide—something I found out from 16 years in the legislature to be a scary prospect.

Women may yet have the last word. Now younger, more diverse, and better educated, they have become an even more important demographic. Suburban women voters were widely credited with the 2018 mid-term victory of the Democrats in retaking the House of Representatives. And black women, especially in the swing states of Pennsylvania and Georgia, have been credited with Joe Biden's victory. Kamala Harris, the first black woman to be nominated as vice president, and Stacey Abrams, a voting-rights activist who narrowly lost the Georgia governor's race in 2018, were key figures in the 2020 campaign.

RBG's legacy energized many other women. In Albuquerque, despite the pandemic, hundreds gathered quickly in the immediate wake of Justice Ginsburg's death to celebrate her life at Tiguex Park near Old Town. The crowd was largely distraught young women. Her memory has not yet faded. In a recent walk along the ditch I saw a handmade sign, tacked to a chain link fence, embellished with feathers, ribbons and wildflowers. It said, "Ruth Bader Ginsburg: May her memory be a blessing, and may we fight like hell to honor her legacy."

Friends of Feldman
Matanza 1999

SENATE DISTRICT 13

The journal today continues a series on legislative candidates in the Nov. 5 general election.

Party affiliation: Democrat

SENATE DISTRICT 13

FELDMAN
STATE SENATE DISTRICT 13

Leader Who Listens

Dale

RE-ELECT SENATOR DEDE FELDMAN
Democrat • June 3, 2008
www.dedefeldman.com

Part II

Most of my politics comes from people who should be famous, but hardly anybody knows their names—people that I've just met in different communities or neighborhoods...who are very inspiring, who have made all the difference...that's what I most believe in.

—Progressive Minnesota
US Senator
Paul Wellstone, 2002

Dear
Thanks for talking with me (or my volunteer) at your home recently. I appreciate your concerns. It's important for a State Senator to listen, and I will call me at 242-1997. I return phone calls! The Democratic Primary is on June 4th & I need your support. Working together, we can win this one for all of us. Your neighbor —
Dede Feldman

9

At Street Level

1996

I HAVE A LIST OF MY TOP TEN MOMENTS AT THE DOOR, some from my first campaign for the senate in 1996 and others from the year before, when I ran for the Albuquerque City Council. I am still figuring out what to do with all those memories. For a while I used the list in speeches to budding campaigners, women who might be afraid to talk to strangers, and burned-out Democrats who do this grunt work for local candidates, rain or shine.

I made my reputation as a street level campaigner. I knew every street in Senate District 13, and before that City Council District 2, most of the North Valley, from Montaño Road south to Old Town, from the river east to I-25. Camilo Lane, that unbelievably narrow, funky street in Duranes, was my favorite because of the preposterous "No Passing" sign. But there is stiff competition from Garden Park Circle and Bayita Lane.

I have trouble covering the territory I once did (about 12-20 houses per hour) when I was younger and more avid, but even now I am still walking the block, knocking on doors, telling people why they should care and why they should vote.

And I still have my clipboard. It's lying idle now, felled by the coronavirus, but it was put to good use in the fall of 2019 when I once again took to the streets to campaign for my city councilor, Ike Benton.

What a weapon. What a tool. The clipboard conveys authority, organization, purpose, intention—plus it can be used to swat pesky dogs who don't always like the door-to-door salesperson, the postal carrier, or the political candidate looking for votes.

The clipboard can be used to cover your head when a rainstorm unexpectedly erupts and you've left your car back at the community center, blocks away. It can hold literature, brochures, and propaganda of all sorts. Most recently, it held a walk list with the names of Democrats on Los Anayas and Gabaldon Roads. Like the paperclip, it's a great retainer (if you don't overstuff it so it spills out all over the porch just when your target audience opens the door).

It didn't help me when I knocked on a door one breezy day near Cochiti Elementary School. Completing a rather satisfactory conversation (I thought) with the homeowner standing in the doorway, I was about to leave some "literature." The homeowner cracked the door, but suddenly a burst of wind blew it hard off the hinges, lifted my skirt to my shoulders and scattered absentee ballot applications all over the yard.

Yet it did help one day when I arrived at a door on San Clemente Avenue at the same time as a door-to-door life insurance salesman. I couldn't believe it. I didn't think there were any left. But there he was, a little gray man with a briefcase and a tie. Guess which one of us the homeowner took notice of? Me—I had the clipboard.

Ten years into my senate stint, in 2008, during the last days of the Obama campaign, two young Brits appeared to get in on the Obama excitement in the final days of the campaign in a Western swing state. One was a member of parliament from Leeds, the other a campaign manager with the Labour Party. They came with me as I knocked on doors in Wells Park. I was so proud of my country and my solidly Democratic district near downtown Albuquerque.

We dropped off our clipboards at the tiny Obama head-quarters on 4th Street, once a pottery studio. The place was packed. Phones were ringing. Everyone had tales from the "hood", mostly about how people were sick of being contacted, again and again, and again. The local Obama campaign manager wanted the Brits to speak about their impressions. I was to give a pep talk about the importance of personal contact in campaigns. The Brits talked about the difference between the presidential and the parlimentary systems— how the Labour Party was similar to the Democratic Party. Yet voters there didn't vote directly for the prime minister but only for their member of parliament. They went door-to-door in Britain too, but the election season was compressed, and candidates didn't spend as much time in the neighbor-hoods.

I talked about how big money was taking over campaigns in the US—but here in New Mexico we were bucking the national trend, with a more grassroots, personal type of campaigning. Relatively small campaigns like mine were still local affairs. Everyone wanted to win, of course, but the stakes were not high enough to completely crucify your opponent, who might live down the street—and whose help you might need one day to fight a landfill or a bridge in your area. But still, campaigns were serious business.

Over time, I had become obsessed with campaigning and not just as a means to an end. As a volunteer, a manager and then as a candidate, campaigns had, for me, become synonymous with community. Okay, well, not the whole community, but damn near. And they were giving me, an only child, a relative stranger in these parts, a larger meaning. Where else do you have an opportunity to meet people with a common purpose, mix it up with folks who are different than you, take risks, and learn about what really happens behind doors that would never normally open to you?

Like the one on Matthew Avenue in 1996.

~

I walked by the house on Matthew Avenue today. It just didn't look the same. The run-down old garage is now attached to the house, and a uniform plaster has been applied to the crumbling white façade that had confronted me, a wannabe senator, in 1996. I was knocking on doors in the neighborhood in search of votes.

I knocked on the door and mentally (and okay, maybe even verbally) practiced my pitch before someone answered the doorbell. "Hi, I'm Dede Feldman. I'm running for office—for the state senate—and I wondered if you had any concerns about the state?"

No answer. I rang again. I knocked. I was preparing to leave and put my "literature" in the door when I heard a voice.

"Running for office? Any concerns?"

It was a strange voice, a spooky, hoarse voice. It was coming from somewhere, but I couldn't figure out where.

"Hello?" I yelled.

"Hello?" it yelled back.

This was truly weird. It seemed to be coming from the garage, off to the side.

Time to leave, I thought, but then it said, "Running for office? Any concerns?"

Oh no, no, no—I'm out of here, I thought, just as a weathered looking man with Depression-era eyes and a gentle face opened the door.

"Yes?" he asked, squinting into the sun, his dirty hair in his eyes. He looked like he had just woken up.

As I started in on my pitch, I heard it again. "Any concerns?"

"I was just about to ask..."

"Any concerns?"

I recognized the voice now. It was the man at the door's. But his lips weren't moving.

Suddenly the homeowner's sad expression broke into a broad grin.

"Oh, that's Marvin," he said. "He's my pet raven. They talk, you know. I trained him to say a few words, but he knows more. Learns 'em from people who come to the door unexpectedly."

We laughed and he offered to introduce me to the raven.

He led me to the garage and opened the door. I looked around. All sorts of hunting equipment was strewn about, fishing tackle piled in the corner, and construction debris everywhere. In the middle there was a covered cage with something moving inside it.

It was Marvin, and as soon as the cover was removed, he cracked opened his thick bill and croaked, "Any concerns?"

The bird was massive, with scruffy feathers that looked eaten. Maybe he had just been in a fight. He was iridescent, his feathers almost blue, and he had dark, dark eyes and talons that gave me pause.

It was my first encounter with someone who kept a wild animal as a pet. The raven had flown away twice, come back once, and the second time the man at the door searched for the bird day and night. He finally found Marvin in a tree in the South Valley. The raven recognized his call.

I'd never thought of animals as being part of my constituency, except maybe in the abstract. But things were beginning to add up in my semi-rural, semi-urban district in Albuquerque's North Valley.

Sure, I'd encountered dogs. Pee Wee, Esse, JoJo, Buster, and Cholo had greeted me at the door on almost every street I walked. I'd been bitten three times. I carried dog yummies and pepper spray. I learned how to put my foot against the screen door so a German shepherd couldn't lunge out before I'd had time to deliver my pitch. And I'd spoken over the yaps, the growls, and the barks to owners who said things like, "Skipper would never bite you."

But ravens? Peacocks? Horses? Donkeys?

"I want you to think carefully about this," a stern older woman in the same neighborhood responded when I asked her about her concerns. "See those horses across the street?"

Dutifully, I acknowledged the Appaloosas, the ponies, and yes, even the donkey across the street. They ran in a pack behind the fence at the end of Meadow View Drive. They smelled up the neighborhood.

I loved the Appaloosas, but I shied away from the ponies after one nipped at me.

"Don't you dare forget about them when you go to Santa Fe," she said. "That's why we're sending you there—to protect them." I could tell from her blunt gray hair and her relentless eye contact that she meant business.

"Yeah," I stumbled around, agreeing all up and down, going on about how we need to protect the environment, and the rural character of the area.

She listened politely. She had heard it all before, and it hadn't made a difference.

I probably couldn't make a difference either, except at the margins. But the two encounters convinced me to sign up for the Senate Conservation Committee, which focused on wildlife, natural resources, the forest, game, fish, and yes, animal protection. Politically, it was not the best perch for an urban newcomer to the senate. But I never regretted it. I got to vote on saving endangered species, protecting the bosque, and preventing water waste and contamination.

Most of the horses are gone now from the field at the end of my street, and spiffy new houses surround the stables backed up against the ditch. I am afraid to knock on the door of the raven man. He's probably dead or old, like me.

But at least I know I did my part for my constituents on Matthew Avenue—all of them.

10

Campaign Relics

1999

For the past nine months in 2020, social gatherings of any size have been banned due to COVID-19. Church services, graduations, reunions, and even funerals are cancelled. It is one of the cruelest symptoms of the virus. Families are separated and rituals disrupted. The ban has been especially hard on politicians, particularly during an election year. By their very nature they are hungry for human contact, the embrace of allies, the wave from the parade float, the thumbs-up signal, and the handshake. I am no different.

Now my dreams are filled with the gatherings that filled my days and nights as a candidate and a senator. I linger at the silver coffee pot at the back of the hotel ballroom as the speaker addresses the group about New Mexico's water debt to Texas. I dip into the buffet of enchiladas or chicken parmesan at the Inn of Loretto, taste the white wine they serve in large glasses at the Rio Chama, and applaud as the environmentalists give out their awards to deserving legislators.

Sometimes the parties of my dreams are outside with speeches on soapboxes. Volunteers come and go with clipboards and pamphlets. There is dancing. A senator from the eastside with whom I drank scotch says, "Can you believe I'm talking to a socialist?" A volunteer does a little jig when the fiddler plays an old tune from northern New Mexico.

Gatherings are symbolic of community and without them we struggle to knit ourselves into a greater whole, into a familiar local fabric, which we need desperately.

For me, as both a campaigner and an elected official, the memory of one particular community gathering is seared in my mind. It is resurrected periodically—not in my dreams—but in my kitchen cabinet and in drawers filled with leftover spices, utensils, and the relics of the biggest campaign party I ever gave.

~

I still have the apron. "Friends of Feldman Matanza 1999," it says, in red script on the bib. It's one of about forty white commercial aprons which I had made for my volunteers to use while they fried chicharrones, cut onions, or stirred the chile at a campaign matanza I held in my backyard twenty years ago as I embarked on my second campaign for the senate. Some of them still may be in circulation but now they are most likely in the grab bag at the Assistance League's thrift store or stuffed into the shopping cart of a homeless person in need of free clothing.

On a bright November morning in 1999, however, scores of volunteers clad in the aprons were out in my backyard, setting up the tent from Garcia's, peeling potatoes, and readying the raffle tickets. One team had stayed late the night before, digging the hole, laying out a lattice of wood at the bottom, lighting the fire underneath, drinking beer, and waiting until the embers were ready for the slabs of beef and the chunks of pork carefully wrapped in tin foil.

The freshly slaughtered pig, from Belen, had hung in the garage for two or three days. My husband, Mark Feldman, a Jew from Brooklyn and neither a butcher nor a hunter, was not happy. But we had been assured by Tom Castillo, now my steadfast ward buddy, that Carl would be here to carve it up in no time. He knew about these things. No problem.

Carl never arrived. Meanwhile, the pig was hanging heavy from the rafters in the adobe garage. Blood was dripping on the concrete floor. It was a chilly November, but still my garage was no icebox. Mark called our neighbor, Andy— God bless him—to help him do the deed usually reserved for butchers. Andy brought his good knives. Mark used the same Sawzall we'd used to build our house.

We served out of the garage. The whole neighborhood— over 200 people—came out. The fire department had been alerted about the fire the night before and the firemen from Station No. 10, on Rio Grande, came too. I saw the Mayor, with whom I was not on particularly good terms, with a spade in hand deep within the matanza hole.

We couldn't afford the traditional mariachis, so we had the Valley High School Spanish band, Los Enamorados, and the Duranes Elementary School choir. Once the festivities got started, Allan Levine (who knew Jews liked matanzas?) asked if he could go home, get his accordion, and stroll among the crowd. He played show tunes—"Hello Dolly," "Some

Enchanted Evening," and "There's No Business Like Show Business."

Other politicians came. There were speeches. Still in my apron, I read a poem about the corner of 12th and Mountain Road, a local landmark. The crowd, not exactly poetry lovers, cheered, then buzzed with memories of old man Duran at the pharmacy, the drawbacks of the Piggly Wiggly grocery store, and what had become of the old Wells Market.

By the time the clean-up crew took over and the tent came down, I knew. These events were the lifeblood of community. They allowed people to check out the inside of your garage, to see that you had the same junk that they did. It allowed them to help out in something they knew how to do much better than you do—choose the right chile, fry chicharrones, season the pork, and slice it as it emerges steaming from its overnight stay in the matanza pit.

They didn't have matanzas in Pennsylvania, where I came from. They had strawberry festivals, pie contests, and smorgasbords. But here in my new home, the North Valley I "got" these parties as family gatherings, Democratic Party rituals, and mini-holidays.

Now, in 2020, as I wash the dishes at the sink in the time of COVID, wearing my dirty, chile-stained apron, I long for gatherings of any kind—graduations, reunions, or ice cream socials. The seniors who attended, often on the arms of their sons or daughters, connected me to the past; their grandchildren connected me to the future—all within a common community with a common purpose.

My daughter Abby is even more party-deprived than I am. Abby has become a special events planner. Her parties have a purpose. She's organized fundraisers for Democratic

candidates in New Mexico, outdoor music festivals to bene-
fit the environment in Arizona, and giant expos to promote
women's wellness in Durango, Colorado. Once she arranged
the quintessential North Valley wedding. It was a giant,
outdoor potluck, with hundreds of guests, long tables, and
five separate bands. Vegetarian, vegan, paleo, lactose intoler-
ant—every diet was accommodated. Instead of elegant party
favors for the guests from the bride and groom, guests took
home garbage bags to compost and recycle the waste.

All along my daughter had been watching the campaigns,
attending the legislative parties, and listening to speeches
at rallies. She has become an avid Democrat, a recycler, an
environmentalist, and a citizen who is building community.

Meanwhile, I remember everything about the matanza—
the diehard vegetarians who only shopped at the Co-op sitting next to the ladies from Our Lady of Guadalupe Church
at the tables we borrowed from the North Valley Senior
Center, the young families, the independent-minded Anglos,
the adventurous do-it-yourselfers for which the North Valley
is famous, the old Italian families, all eating cake and talking
about Monica Lewinsky or Ralph Garcia, the prison guard
who had been killed at that private prison in Santa Rosa a
few weeks earlier.

There, too, were my Hispanic neighbors who had adopted me and my husband back in the 1970s as we mixed mud
and laid adobes in the hot sun, adding a solar greenhouse to
a small house that looked a lot like theirs. They are the ones
who gave me, once an outsider, the courage to do this, to run
for office, to lose once, to run again, and to win.

11

Election Day

June 1996

I WAS STILL OUT ON THE MEDIAN STRIP on Rio Grande Boulevard, the one that the homeless hang out on, near I-40. I was waving the last of my yard signs, forcing a smile, pantomiming the directions to the nearby polling place when I heard the bell from St. Francis de Neri toll seven times. The polls were now closed. Primary Election 1996 was over.

I was too tired to quit. The effort it would take to shift gears was too much and the exhausted aftermath, no matter the outcome, was terrifying. Finally, someone pulled me away. I can't remember whether it was Tom Castillo or Sam Garcia. Or maybe it was Spider. Spider was there, until the very end. He waved his large, dirty bandana in circles around his head, crying "*Oye! Oye! Oye!*" like a combination town crier and mariachi.

I was never one to let up on election day. Some candidates, knowing things were beyond their control, went to the movies or had their nails done. But I made every last call

I could. I knocked on doors, offered rides, and made myself larger than life at polling places. There was still time.

By the time I got back to the house, which served as my campaign headquarters, volunteers were putting down their phone lists, icing the drinks, and readying the barbeque for the crowd. The tally sheets were posted, awaiting the first returns. The TVs were set up and someone had turned on KANW radio's election-night coverage. It was Joe Monahan with all talk, but no returns.

We had sent runners to each polling place to collect the results directly, and they were beginning to come in from Duranes Elementary, Valley High School, and Wells Park Community Center. The volunteers, the door-to-door knockers, the phone bankers, the yard-sign erectors, and the faithful contributors crowded around the white, butcher block paper posted on the closet door in Mark's studio. It looked good, but it was still too early to tell, so we retreated to get some food from the table outside. No luck. The red and green chile from Monroe's was all gone; and so was the barbeque. We should have known. Democrats eat everything in sight.

Just then a noise came from inside. My campaign manager, John Gastil, whom we called "The Professor," was yelling. All night he had been at the computer, comparing the actual results with his projections for each precinct. He was smiling. "A victory for social science! A victory for social science!" he yelled. Before all the results were in, he knew I had won. I believed him. John was not the usual up-and-coming young politico in training for his own race. No, John was from the university, a believer in data, in careful record keeping, and in computer lists. Sometimes he closed his eyes when he talked because he was thinking so hard.

The volunteers who had given it their all wanted to see the actual count. They had stood with me circulating petitions outside John Brooks and J. Michael's supermarkets, walked in parades in Dietz Farms and Matthew Meadows with corny signs, knocked on door after door, endured chihuahuas and chows, and danced with dubious characters at the North Valley Senior Center. They had been disappointed before. The year before I had lost my race for the city council by a heartbreaking nine votes. They wanted to be sure.

Soon it was undeniable. I had won almost every precinct. The areas I did the best were where I had walked repeatedly in some of the heavily Hispanic neighborhoods. Retail politics had worked. My leap of faith—and our hard work—had been rewarded.

Soon my opponent, Virginia Trujillo, called to concede. Several of her volunteers, still wearing Trujillo T-shirts, joined our celebration. We would work together in the general election, which, as everyone knew, was a slam-dunk for the Democrats.

And then, the speech. My first thanks went to my husband, Mark, who had encouraged me, and put up with this, the latest of my projects. He had put up signs, gone door-to-door, something only I knew he hated. Then, my thanks went to my first allies, the women who had come to my side early when the politicos had hesitated, hedging their bets, not sure a woman, a progressive, or an Anglo could win in a Democratic primary.

I looked around. It was the same room, and mostly the same people, but everything was different from the gathering that occurred there a few months earlier in October of 1995, when I had lost my bid for the city council. Now there was no uncomfortable hush, no uncertainty, no recount, and no final speech. Yet, without that first night, this one could not have happened.

By the time I had won the Democratic primary in June of 1996, I had walked almost every street in the North Valley, from Montaño south to Central and from the river on the west to I-25 on the east. I had been bitten by dogs. I had lost 20 pounds, spoken to homemakers at kitchen tables covered in oilcloths, and waited politely when tough guys washing their cars in the driveway wouldn't stop to talk. I bought lemonade from the neighborhood kids every chance I got, and I went inside when I shouldn't have. I wrote thank you notes to every person I spoke with. I returned every phone call. My first instinct was right. If I simply got to know people in person, they would see that I was not a threat. Now I knew the community—its fears, hopes, complaints, jokes, habits, tastes, and hot buttons. And they knew me—my progressive tendencies, my story, my volunteers, and my plans for reform. They had allowed me to put up yard signs right in front of their houses. They tipped me off about events I should attend—a church fiesta or a family reunion. And they trusted me with their vote.

I vowed to pay them back.

My newfound community, with its liberal and tolerant spirit, would sustain me for sixteen years as I grew as a public servant. But it was the magic, the ups and downs, and the synchronicity of my initial door-to-door campaigns, first for the city council in 1995, and then for the state senate in 1996, that made me into the senator that I became.

For about a year, I had been a street person, on foot, without a car, armed only with a clipboard. I saw things I had never noticed, although they had been there all along. I smelled the horses on Matthew Avenue, right in the middle of the city, and saw kids throwing rocks into the ditches. I knew what time the mail was delivered in the Corley Homes addition, and whether the trash had been picked up on Thursday. I discovered a tower of sneakers, a street-side art gallery on Camilo Lane, and heard the sound of the Valley High School band practicing. I saw countless old cars parked in front yards waiting for a missing part. I even got into one to talk to a lonely veteran whose wife had died. I smelled the green chile roasting and saw families gathering to peel off the skin. Sometimes I would hear the sandhill cranes calling and lift my eyes to follow their v-shaped formations as they made their way south.

The houses facing the streets I had driven along for years now had inhabitants I knew—the Garcia family on Rio Grande Boulevard and the Roybals on Griegos. I had seen what was in the backyards, out of view—a giant Buddha behind a modest home on Candelaria, an illegal mother-in-law dwelling on San Lorenzo, a treehouse on Los Arboles, or a sweat lodge off Rio Grande.

I had never bothered much with the details of ordinary life. I thought I had better things to do or things to accomplish on a higher level. Now I listened, I watched, and learned about the lives of ordinary people who became extraordinary, and in some cases even heroic to me. The stories I heard during that year—stories of hardship, of success, of mental illness, and religious belief—stuck with me and formed the backdrop of the policies I promoted and the laws I made in the New Mexico Senate.

12

Ten More Doors

2004

I STILL HAD TEN MORE FAMILIES TO CONTACT on Cherokee Avenue east of Valley High School. But it was getting dark and if I had one ironclad rule about canvassing it was not to knock on voters' doors after nightfall. It creates a bad impression.

There was only one thing to do—run. I might be able to make my self-imposed quota if people didn't talk too much. But of course they did. That was the whole point of canvassing.

Some candidates I had helped just shoved the flyer into the person's hand and said, "Hi, I'm so-and-so and I'm running for office and I hope you'll vote for me. I live here in the area." But ever since my first campaign I had touted myself as the senator who listens. Every year, right before the legislative session I sent out a detailed questionnaire to frequent voters, and my pitch at the door was, "Do you have any concerns about state government?"

Maybe the last few people on the list wouldn't be home, or I wouldn't be able to find the door. I was always surprised by the number of new houses which had absolutely no access to the street. The entrance was only through the garage, through a locked patio gate or around back through the yard with the vicious Rottweiler. No chance of spontaneous interactions and no contribution to the public space in front of the home.

But *running*? This must be a desperate holdover from when I lost my first campaign by nine votes. What was I thinking?

A couple of times I had tripped when I was just walking, sorting through maps and lists as I tried to figure out where to go next. Once, blood ran down my chin from where the clipboard had hit my face. It was in the Wells Park neighborhood, and the next person whose door I knocked on took me in and gave me a wet paper towel.

I had no excuse for the bizarre impressions I made at the door. Sometimes I would get caught jumping the fence at a gated community or my cell phone would go off just as the door opened. Once, when I was asking someone to sign a petition for me to get on the ballot, I drooled on the petition just as I was handing it to the resident. She signed it anyway.

Other times I stepped in it, especially when my Spanish skills were put to a test. The smell of a wonderful chocolate cake wafting from a kitchen would spur me to say, "*Caca chocolata, muy bueno aqui.*" When an English-speaking relative gently explained the mistake (*caca* does not mean "cake" in Spanish, but feces), I'd say "Oh, *soy muy embarazada,*" which means "I'm so pregnant."

I must have knocked on thousands of doors over the years and engaged in—even encouraged—hundreds of incoherent conversations, all on the theory that if people got to know me, they might see that—even though I was a woman, not from here, and not Hispanic—I posed no threat.

Most of the last people that night were not at home, but at one house the porch light was on, so I knocked. A woman came to the door who had a developmentally disabled son. We talked about the long waiting list for services and how hopeless it seemed for aging parents who wondered what would happen to their adult children when they died.

I told her every year the legislature put in a few more million to take people off the list and provide services, but it never seemed to be enough. Maybe the system was flawed, I suggested. The problem had gone on for years.

She shook her head. I felt powerless, more powerless than when I had come to the legislature knowing nothing about the problem. In the eight years that I had been there, the more I knew, the worse I felt.

But somehow, Rose—I think that was her name—forgave me. She knew I had sponsored bills about autism, tried to preserve Medicaid, and get higher salaries for the people who worked at group homes and sheltered workshops. Turns out she worked at the Adelante Development Center. But it didn't come up that night.

As I walked back to my car, exhausted, I thought about Rose and something that had happened the night before, in a front yard crowded with tricycles, plastic slides, and a kiddie pool. The woman who came to the door was older than Rose and older than me. She was raising her grandchildren. The strain was showing. The worry lines in her forehead deepened as she told me how she couldn't register one child for kindergarten because she didn't have custody, and the other kids didn't have a doctor because Medicaid wouldn't cover them without parental consent. She was not the first grandparent I met in the same situation. Duranes seemed to be full of grandparents raising their children's children.

Mandy Goodyear invited me into her house on Iris Road NW and introduced me to her severely disabled granddaughter, then receiving some in-home therapy from an occupational therapist. I had never heard of an occupational therapist, never knew the load that some women carried, just by the luck of the draw.

Where were the parents? At first I was too polite to ask. But the more I got to know the North Valley, at street level, it became clear. Our neighbors' children were struggling with addiction, were incarcerated, or worse.

Not in my neighborhood, I thought. But then I remembered. My own next-door neighbor raised her grandchild, Gilbert, while her daughter was in prison, and later after she died of a drug overdose. When things got too hard, she sent him to the Boys' Ranch down in Valencia County. After he came back, I went to his wedding. He survived.

I would do all I could to see that the grandparents and their grandchildren survived as well. It was a vow I took on the sidewalks, too late at night, in the wrong neighborhoods, talking too much. The result, once I got to the legislature, was in the bills I was able to pass: the Kinship Guardianship Act and the Foster Grandparents Program, both of which gave grandparents rights; the Brain Injury Services Fund; senior prescription drug discounts; and funding for developmental disabilities services and the people who provide them.

Senate Panel Backs Graduated Licenses

Advocates Say Measure
May Save Teen Drivers

New law expands
grandparents' legal
rights and speeds
guardianship of kin

Part III

Ours is not the struggle of one day, one week, or one year. Ours is not the struggle of one judicial appointment or presidential term. Ours is the struggle of a lifetime, or maybe even many lifetimes, and each of us in every generation must do our part.

—Georgia US Representative
John Lewis,
Across that Bridge:
A Vision for Change and the
Future of America (2012)

13

First Days in
the Senate

January 1997

"THIS IS CRAZY," SHE SAID, WITH THE ALARM of a mother confronting her teenager's dangerous behavior. "You've got to slow down. Pace yourself. You can't do everything." Senator Pauline Eisenstadt had observed me closely during my first week in the New Mexico Senate. She saw my flurry of bill introductions, my meetings with the Attorney General, and my attendance at parties thrown by lobbyists in ballrooms all over Santa Fe.

Pauline had been there before, serving eight years in the New Mexico House before she was elected to the senate in 1997, the same year as I was. Now we were office mates, along with four other senators on the first floor of the Roundhouse near the east entrance. The women's bathroom was directly across the hall and the curved corridor was always crowded with school kids just off the bus from Moriarty or Thoreau. The voices of children on their way to the nearby senate gallery provided a permanent soundtrack. Sometimes high school mariachis would tune up outside our door.

"You'll get sick," she warned, looking for affirmation from Senator Cisco McSorley or Senator Linda Lopez, our two freshmen officemates.

I didn't pay any attention. I had found my element. The people I had met at the door in the North Valley during the campaign were just the beginning. Here were Navajos, like my neighbors on the chamber's floor, to my right and my left—Senator Leonard Tsosie, from Crownpoint, and Senator John Pinto, from Tohatchi. Courtly gentlemen in cowboy hats from the East Side introduced themselves with a flourish. The women legislators were dressed to the hilt, with hats, turquoise, silver necklaces or tailored suits with corsages. There was laughter and jokes. A reunion of some kind going on in the lobby. Wow, these people were as interested in politics as I was.

I was elated.

In grade school, grown-ups would always ask, "What do you want to be when you grow up?" It was a common question for kids growing up during the 1950s, when the sky was the limit. I was torn between becoming a medical missionary, which my mother, a fan of Albert Schweitzer, favored, or president, one like JFK, whom my father pointed out had more power. I wasn't religious enough for missionary work, so I stuck with president, and my sixth-grade yearbook recorded it as my ambition. They said my destiny, however, was to be a waitress. They had never heard of Alexandria Ocasio-Cortez, a waitress in New York before she entered Congress.

By my senior year in high school my priorities were clear. I joined the debate team. I flipped through endless 3"x 5" cards with facts for or against a Medicare program or the Nuclear Test Ban Treaty. Blue was pro; pink was con. Civil rights was more important to me than the Beatles—I knew that. I couldn't get enough of the era's dramatic events— Martin Luther King's "Letter from Birmingham Jail," the Selma-to-Montgomery march, Medgar Evers's murder. Every afternoon my father brought home *The Philadelphia Evening Bulletin* (he worked there) along with *The New York Times* and sometimes *The Washington Post.* I wanted to go south with the Freedom Riders, but I didn't dare ask my parents. I was only 14. I knew Quaker teenagers from my area who went. I ached to join them.

Then, there was the family tradition. My great aunt was the county clerk in Chester County, Pennsylvania, at a time when few women held that position, and my grandfather ran for county treasurer. His father, James Whitcraft, an avid Democrat, died on the courthouse steps making a speech praising Andrew Jackson—a spectacularly bad choice. My family included both Democrats and Republicans. Everyone liked President Eisenhower and then Kennedy.

It was in my blood. My Pennsylvania ancestors had fought for independence from the British and spent the winter at Valley Forge. Later, their Quaker schools were part of the Underground Railroad. There was never a time I was not interested in politics, but I didn't actually do anything about it until the 1960s when issues of civil rights and Vietnam threw me—and my whole generation—into the streets to protest injustice and war.

In November of 1965, I traveled to Washington, D.C., to join one of the first anti-war marches that would mark the next decade. I wore my lumberjacket and my alligator boots, the ones like the girl on the cover of *The Freewheelin' Bob Dylan* album wore. My first sight of the crowd, 50,000 strong, almost knocked me over with the intensity of thousands, the sound of bongos, the smell of patchouli oil, and the smoke from college cigarettes rising. I didn't know which direction to go. Mothers were pushing baby carriages with signs saying, "Stop the Bombing." Organizers with clipboards pressed me to sign petitions; veterans in uniform were making the peace sign and posing for photos.

There were throngs of college students in worn-out pea jackets, boots, and dark eyeshadow—just like me. Hundreds of buses from New England, Michigan, and the Midwest arrived regularly and disgorged their eager passengers at the Washington Monument. Giant papier mâché puppets portraying "General WasteMoreLand" popped up in the crowd. Signs said, "Bring the Troops Home." The sound of distant chants rose, then fell. "Hey, hey LBJ, how many kids did you kill today?" Just then I heard some familiar melodies. Pete Seeger and Joan Baez were singing in small groups, scattered among the crowd. These were my heroes from records I listened to in my college dorm, and at a coffee house I once went to in Philadelphia. They were not solitary voices. Others had heard the call and heeded them here in the shadow of the Capitol. Phil Ochs bellowed out, "I Ain't Marching Anymore." Maybe the song was for the veterans I had seen earlier—boys, even younger than I was, who would bear the entire burden of war, answer the moral questions that I didn't have to face just because I was a girl.

Nearby, conscientious objectors, socialists, and longhairs argued about the best way to end the war. On the podium, someone I had actually met before, Carl Oglesby, spoke. I recognized his red hair. He was a leader of SDS, the Students for a Democratic Society, which had organized the whole thing.

It was the first mass mobilization. More Washington demonstrations would follow. Another in the spring and many more the next year. Crowds swelled to 100,000 and then 200,000—even more in New York and on the West Coast. Bob Dylan's "The Times They Are a Changing" played on the radio. Draft cards burned. In Washington, one group circled the Pentagon. Another, which I joined, lobbied individual congresspeople, with help from the Women's International League for Peace and Freedom and the War Resisters League.

It began for me there, in November of 1965—a glimpse of a whole new world where change was possible. Here were young, old, well-heeled, scruffy, Black, White, and Native American people all joining together to make something happen. Something important. They were complete strangers to me, yet I felt a bond, a unity across the states, across the boundaries of race and class. That first glimpse of the crowd on that November morning let loose a thousand little pinpricks all over my body—behind my eyes, at the tips of my fingers, on the soles of my feet. I wanted to cry and smile at the same time. Suddenly, my skin was red. I was tingling all over. I was in love, or maybe it was like being "saved," walking to the front of the church, making the commitment to Jesus. Some long-buried synapses in my brain had connected. The confines of my proper education and my narrow Pennsylvania upbringing were broken. I was hooked. I wanted that feeling again. I searched for it everywhere. Finally, the search brought me to the New Mexico Senate.

~

I still remember the January day I drove up to Santa Fe from Albuquerque to get my office set up. I had bills to draft. The Attorney General wanted to meet with me about our tobacco bill. Volunteers from my campaign were coming up for my swearing in. There was a party planned at my favorite restaurant, Tortilla Flats.

There was magic in the air. An old friend from Santa Fe, Dotty Davis, offered to let me stay in the little apartment attached to her main house, off of West Alameda. My contractor husband had built it for her a few years earlier. It was her contribution to my efforts, she said. Others came forward to help with things I didn't know I needed. People started calling me "Senator."

Now I was ready to get behind the mule and plow. I researched cigarette sales to minors and how to stop them, how to limit the size of campaign contributions so special interests were not buying elections. I sought funds to help people with traumatic brain injuries. I revised my bill creating a Bosque Council to make multi-jurisdictional decisions to save the endangered riparian forest along the Rio Grande. I was on the phone constantly, reading biological opinions, federal court cases, lining up expert witnesses, and getting the language of the bills right.

"I never saw her so fully engaged," Mark told friends, "Body, mind and soul. It's what she's been waiting for."

I did my homework every night. I read all the bills and all the analyses from the Legislative Finance Committee. I tried to master every detail just as I had tried to learn every detail about the history of Vietnam, the fallacy of the domino theory, how Dow Chemical made napalm, and who were the hawks and who were the doves in Congress. I answered all my mail, even if the sender was not from my district. I hired a secretary for the first time in my life and tried to figure out what to do with her. In keeping with senate tradition, I got to hire an attendant. Mine was a recent graduate from Harvard, who did far more than the others, who typically opened doors to the chamber or leaned against the paneled walls. I would be different.

That first year, I introduced twenty bills. They were all substantive. Most veterans will tell you to focus on one or two, or even refrain from introducing any, until you get the lay of the land. But I had gotten a late start. I was 50. I had to make up for lost time.

My first big bill was related to the place I came from, the North Valley. In retrospect, I see it as part of my continuing saga of advances, retreats, zigzags, and circles around the big issues that possessed me. I had always wanted to do my part to protect the bosque, which ran through my district like a verdant green ribbon. It provided a connection with nature for urban dwellers and a home for the porcupines, beavers, and hawks who lived there. The bosque was one of the largest urban cottonwood forests in the country and it was within walking distance for nearly everyone in the North Valley, including me.

There was a problem, though. The bosque was not healthy. The cottonwoods were all approximately the same age, and new growth just wasn't happening since flooding from the Rio Grande was no longer a regular occurrence. Starting in the 1930s, man-made structures like levees had been constructed to prevent the flooding of downtown Albuquerque. A dam was built upstream. Now, with less rainfall, there was not enough water. Restoring the bosque was a problem that demanded active river management.

With the zeal of a freshman, I sponsored a bill that would bring together river managers, users, municipalities, advocates, and federal and state agencies from up and down the Rio Grande to coordinate decisions on river flow, fire management, and recreation—all with the goal of preserving the majestic cottonwoods.

I met strangers who would become my heroes—people like Bill deBuys, a naturalist and writer who had written a cultural history of the Sangre de Cristo mountain range and personified it in his book *River of Traps*. It is hard to overstate the power of the stories that this elegant narrator used to crystalize complex natural phenomenon. Metaphors and analogies filled his testimony about global warming or overgrazing. The drying of the Rio Grande was a symbol of the West's decline, he said. Political inaction was more dangerous than natural catastrophe. His words flew over the heads of busy legislators, or sparked opposition from those who were against anything that smacked of environmentalism. Later, I would work with Bill for over a decade to preserve the Valles Caldera, an iconic landscape in the heart of the Jemez Mountains. We were ultimately successful.

One afternoon, another new ally showed up in my office, introducing himself as a "river boy." He was a shaggy, weather-beaten man who smelled like cigarettes and looked like he had just camped out overnight. He had. It was Steve Harris, the founder of Rio Grande Restoration and the owner of Far Flung Adventures, a river rafting outfit out of Taos. Harris knew everything the scientists had learned from a book—from being on the river day after day, navigating its high and low flows, spotting endangered species, and overgrazed riverbanks.

I spent hours on the phone with Cliff Crawford, a UNM biologist who knew even more. I read his *Bosque Biological Management Plan* cover to cover, dug into documents from the Bureau of Reclamation, the U.S. Fish and Wildlife Service, and court decisions on endangered species like the silvery minnow. Cliff died several years ago, but not before marshalling a young army of students and citizen scientists to study and restore the bosque under the banner of the Bosque Environmental Monitoring Project (BEMP). Long after I left the senate, I wrote about this model program in *Another Way Forward: Grassroots Solutions from New Mexico.*

Who knew that biology was such a political issue?

Soon I saw that one thing was related to another. Before I knew it, I was studying the Rio Grande, the water debt we owed Texas, the drought, Western water wars, and climate change. It was a crash course that reminded me of my college courses about Vietnam and the Mekong Delta. My bill, Senate Bill 879 to establish the Bosque Council, passed that year. I was ecstatic.

Governor Gary Johnson, a Republican, promptly vetoed it. I couldn't believe it. I had done everything right. I had bipartisan support. Republican Senator Joe Carraro, whose westside district included part of the bosque, was on board. He lobbied the Governor along with hundreds of others. Larry Lattman, a former president of New Mexico Tech, visited the Governor personally. Bill deBuys had even secured private funding to operate the Council from Suzy Poole, a wealthy woman whose westside home was nestled in the bosque.

The process taught me what it was like to work with a big, bipartisan, statewide coalition and mobilize a citizen lobbying campaign. It brought me back to another decade when the citizens of Senate District 13 opposed the Montaño bridge, and after years of struggle, lost.

Oh my, another loss, this one right from the start. This did not bode well. Memories of all the elections I had lost—my own bid for the city council a few years earlier, and those of my allies, candidates like Brant Calkin, Pat Baca, and others who had come so close—flooded my mind. But then I remembered, losing was not the end of the world. Sometimes there are consolation prizes—if you don't walk away in despair or anger.

A few months after the legislative session, just as I was thinking that all my efforts—the coalition I had built, the research I had done, the new allies I had gained—were for naught, I got a call. It was from Jennifer Salisbury, then the Secretary of the Energy, Minerals and Natural Resources Department (EMNRD), telling me the administration had decided to set up a "Bosque Consortium" to deliberate on issues concerning the bosque. It was exactly the same thing that I had proposed, and the Governor had vetoed. They had co-opted the whole idea! Some nerve. Salisbury asked me to be on it, and then went even further. Would I fund it with the private funding that Bill deBuys had obtained? I said no to the funding, but yes to the Consortium.

A straight line is not always the shortest distance between two points. I was beginning to understand. Losses on the big issues may be inevitable, given bureaucratic inertia, lack of funding, special interests, or the ample supply of reasons to resist any change. But the process—assembling the coalition, educating the public and the legislature—built power for the next campaign. My other big bill of the 1997 session, a public health measure to license the retail sellers of tobacco products in order to control cigarette sales to minors, was also vetoed that year. In 2020, the same bill finally passed. Neither the environmentalists nor the anti-cancer activists had given up, scoring significant victories in the meantime.

In the next few years, the deliberations of the Bosque Consortium shaped an unexpected consensus on how to clear parts of the bosque in order to preserve the whole. Some of the fire management techniques were used in fighting the huge bosque fire that raged to the west of my own house in 2003. The restoration and fire prevention efforts continue today. And the ball is still advancing down the field.

Groups Come Together To Keep Bosque Healthy

Consortium Result Of Johnson Order

BY TANIA SOUSSAN
Journal Staff Writer

With a sponsor on board, a new organization charged with preserving the bosque is ready to get down to work.

The Middle Rio Grande Council of Governments agreed last week to act as coordinator for a regional "bosque consortium" that will bring together pueblos, government agencies and other groups that deal with river management between Cochiti and Elephant Butte.

"It's sort of a United Nations of the Rio Grande," said Sen. Dede Feldman, D-Albuquerque. "It doesn't have any formal power, but it has the power of persuasion, and it has the public eye."

The consortium was created as a result of an executive order from Gov. Gary Johnson. A similar pro-

FELDMAN: "A United Nations of the Rio Grande"

U.S. Fish and Wildlife Service, the state Energy, Minerals & Natural Resources Department and other state agencies.

"We're going to try to draw as many people into it as possible," Feldman said. Dozens of government entities have jurisdiction along various stretches of the Rio Grande.

The consortium will meet several times a year to discuss flooding practices, riverside clean-up and other initiatives to preserve a healthy bosque, Feldman said.

The next step will be for the Council of Governments to coordinate an initial meeting and possibly pin down a structure and funding for the effort.

14

Lessons in Loyalty

2001

I CANNOT ERASE CERTAIN MEMORIES connected with the 2001 legislative session: the screaming diatribes of Senator Shannon Robinson, the tears of Senator Mary Kay Papen, the mock trial atmosphere of the Senate Rules Committee as it considered redistricting, or the open hostility focused on me by members of the Democratic caucus because I was an Anglo who represented a Hispanic community. All were connected to one central event—the overthrow of our brilliant, swashbuckling President Pro Tempore Manny Aragon. It was by far the most dramatic scene in my sixteen years in the New Mexico Senate.

There had been rumblings of discontent ever since the Senate Pro Tem took a lobbying contract with Wackenhut Corrections Corporation (now the GEO Group), the builder of private prisons. Even so, the razor-thin vote to depose Manny Aragon sent a shock wave through the Capitol in Santa Fe that year. Longtime aides went running from the chamber in disbelief. A fight nearly broke out between Senator Shannon Robinson and Senator Leonard Tsosie. A dramatic silence seized the floor.

It was inconceivable that the passionate master of the senate, the "boy wonder" turned tactician extraordinaire, had fallen.

The final vote was 21 to 20 for Senator Richard Romero, a mild-mannered educator from Albuquerque. I had kept my promise to Manny and voted for him rather than Romero, who won with the votes of eighteen Republicans and two maverick Democrats who dared to break ranks with their party—Senators Cisco McSorley and Leonard Tsosie. It was the politic thing to do, I thought. In the New Mexico Senate your word is your bond. I had explained it to Richard, who knew the rule and somehow forgave me. A relatively new senator, I wanted so much to be a part of the Democratic team, even if the team was not so much a team as a rubber stamp. At least it was a rubber stamp for the liberal values I held dear. Or so I told myself.

Today's Republican senators in Washington line up to protect the outlandish abuses served up by Donald Trump. Yesterday's Democratic partisans in the New Mexico Senate stood in solid support of their leader of 13 years. Even when his personal attacks, his bullying, and his sharp reversals left them hanging, they didn't mind. They said no one could do the budget like Manny. No one could hold forth on the floor in defense of people with disabilities or people whose only sin was to be Hispanic or poor. He was a strategic genius, a chess master with daring plans. He knew each of the senators personally, the needs of their districts, their pet projects, their weaknesses, and their wives. It was part of his power.

After the vote all hell broke loose. Egged on by Manny, the Democrats declared war. Richard Romero, who had become the new Pro Tem, was the subject of heated attack. A live grenade was thrown at him—procedurally, verbally—every day on the floor of the senate. Even the least controversial matters—committee reports or approval of routine motions—were contentious. Every senator had a rulebook at the ready. Senator Shannon Robinson, Manny's ally, was not afraid of name-calling. Tsosie was a "birdbrain;" McSorley was "bald and ugly." Romero was a Benedict Arnold. "The traitor had no shame in his betrayal," Robinson repeated over and over whenever there was a lull in the action.

Richard took the abuse with equanimity. He must have been trained in passive, non-violent resistance. He responded with silence, which infuriated his opponents, who then began calling him "the invisible man."

Once I saw what was going on, I vowed to help Richard in any way I could. I hadn't voted for him and was more philosophically aligned with the progressive Aragon, but I was relieved Richard was elected. And I was ashamed that I didn't have the courage to vote for him. He was sticking up for the process—the rules of the game—that Aragon had repeatedly swept aside in his quest for power.

Contrary to Democratic predictions, Romero was not a sell-out. He did not appoint Republicans to become committee chairs. Nor did he give up his principles, which included voting rights for felons, one of his bills that session. He simply tried to create order out of chaos and return fairness to committees and budget making, which had become travesties of the legislative process. Until then, Manny controlled the budget and gave directions to the finance committee from a small scrap of paper kept in the pocket of his double-breasted navy blazer. He appointed the chairs of committees without consultation from the Committee on Committees. Opponents, or members of the administration who testified before committees on which he sat, were humiliated. Their physical appearances were belittled. Their abilities demeaned. He introduced over 50 bills per session, pushing them through the senate singlehandedly, holding bills hostage, trading off favors with house members to get them through the process. Whether it was in fear or complicity, the senate Democrats, by and large, sat silent.

Romero, an athlete who had played college baseball and flag football with Manny back in Barelas, the Albuquerque barrio where they both grew up, had a favorite analogy for the situation. It revolved around basketball. "Why should one person be the one who controls the ball, makes all the passes, and takes all the shots? There's a whole team out there with talents," he said. Romero thought that many of the Democrats had been stifled all those years and left with little decision-making power. He thought, ultimately, they would step up to new responsibilities.

After the fateful vote, Manny's allies, the "true" Democrats, resorted to sabotage, overthrowing any non-believers in a secret Democratic caucus and working hard to sink the budget to prove that only Manny was capable of formulating a plan to run state government.

They were not successful.

What eventually unfolded restored my faith in the process. The Senate Finance Committee came forth with a fair budget under the leadership of Senator Ben Altamirano and some brave committee members who rose to the occasion to support it.

Gradually other members of the senate, who had given up thinking on their own and relied on Manny to tell them how to vote, began to make up their own minds. A hundred flowers bloomed.

I was one of them.

In the new senate, voting was not always on party lines. I was able to pass more bills—even controversial ones, like requiring trigger locks for guns. The old oaths of absolute loyalty began to fade. Issues were taken one at a time, voted on their own merit. The next year, the new Pro Tem appointed me chairperson of the Public Affairs Committee, a post I held for ten years. It was not so much a reward for my loyalty, since I had not been there when it counted, but a symbolic move toward good government and fairness. I was already known for my efforts to clean up campaigns and promote ethics. I served, I suppose, as counterpoint to the previous chair. He had been notorious for erratic behavior and scorn toward all those who crossed him or his buddies from the tobacco, alcohol, and pharmaceutical lobbies.

The hostility in the Senate Democratic Caucus went on and on. For all of 2001 there was no middle ground. You had to choose one side or the other. None of the usual fraternization was permitted—only formalities, conspiratorial huddles, and secret conversations in the restroom. Floor votes were a referendum on either Manny or Richard—the issue be damned. Everything had broken down. The Democrats were eating themselves alive. We knew it but continued anyway.

For years, a fair process had not mattered. Manny had taken care of us. We got the capital outlay we needed for our districts and our priorities for increased minimum wages, better health care, and human rights advanced. It would have worked except for the executive branch occupied by a Republican governor. But it was a cycle. The Governor's resistance then became a reason for even more draconian legislative methods.

Writing this now, recently living through Trump and his allies in the US Senate, it all seems so obvious. The rules of the game are thwarted regularly by a president who has no regard for democratic principles (with a small, not a capital, "D"). The authority of the courts, the facts, ethics, and the sanctity of fair elections all were meaningless, unless they advanced his personal agenda.

Under the leadership of Mitch McConnell, the US Senate reminds me of the New Mexico Senate of the 1990s. The Republican senators know better, but they are willing to go along with anyone who will allow them to remain in power and achieve their partisan goals. We've heard their excuses: "Oh, it's just Trump being Trump," or, "I haven't actually seen that tweet, so I can't comment." Suddenly the senators scatter when asked about the latest outrage.

Meanwhile, in the name of the President, their leader has led them into breaking the longstanding rules of the game—holding no hearings on obvious abuses of executive power, allowing no witnesses in an impeachment trial, sitting by while the executive refuses congressional supoenas, manipulating the confirmation of Supreme Court justices to delay—and then rush—to fill the Court with Republican partisans.

The longer it goes on, the harder it becomes for them to resist. US senators have been forced to swallow bigger and bigger lies, more acts of outright corruption, more firings, more racial dog whistles, calls to violence, betrayals of foreign allies, even infringement on their own power. There have been few profiles in courage among the senators in the majority.

It's hard to stand up to bullies, I found, even for senators, especially when things are going well and your leader is pursuing the things you want: a living wage, higher teacher salaries, and services for women, children, and people with low incomes. Yes, Manny was moving the ball down the field in the right direction faster than most leaders. But there was something wrong, something corrupt about taking bills hostage, damaging the reputation of any who oppose you, and bending the rules. I recoiled every time he insulted officials from the Department of Health as "stupid" or "racist." I winced when he threatened to defeat bills based on the sponsor being too elitist, or from a part of the state he didn't like.

Maybe strong-arm tactics always work. They certainly did in Amin's Uganda. I knew that. But this is a democratic society with checks and balances, a free press, the rule of law, and elections. Maybe I was a sucker, but I still believed in these things. Finally, in 2007, the once powerful Pro Tem was indicted in a Metropolitan Courthouse scandal. He pled guilty to siphoning off $600,000 from $4.2 million in funds he had sponsored while in the legislature. He served four and a half years in federal prison in Colorado. The rule of law had finally come into play.

Manny had his enablers, his apologists, and his beneficiaries, just as Mitch McConnell, Donald Trump, and Idi Amin did. These enablers excused Manny's language, his attacks, his late nights, and his imperious decisions. He had a plan, they said. He can pull rabbits out of a hat. "Gotta give him credit for sheer brilliance," one senator said.

But there were also courageous senators who risked everything to stand up for the system as well as for democratic values. Richard Romero was one of them. I once asked him how he did it. "I don't really know," he said, "I was just fed up and felt like I had nothing to lose." Romero's acknowledgment that there are some things more important than short-term political gain remains lost on many politicians, but his courage was an inspiration to me as I served in the New Mexico Senate.

15

Stump Speech

1995-2019

I HAVE A SOAPBOX SET UP IN MY BACKYARD where politicians have given their stump speeches to potential donors, supporters, and constituents. Tom Udall, Tim Keller, Diane Denish, Richard Romero, Martin Heinrich, and Jim Baca have all given their pitches while standing on it. It's a requirement. Speakers have decried global warming or tax breaks for the rich from it. Some have laid out plans to crack down on crime or proposed education reforms. A tray of wine glasses crashed to the flagstone as John Edwards explored the widening gap between the rich and the poor. Bill Richardson waved a swollen hand and begged off from the traditional glad-handing. He had just come from the New Mexico State Fair, where he had earned an entry in *The Guinness Book of World Records* for shaking the most hands in one day.

Mine is a Democratic household, but the soapbox, and the political speech it implies is a democratic tradition— with a small "d." Labor firebrands, anarchists, Tories, and suffragettes have all used the box—often when more expensive means of communication are closed. My father, serving in England during WWII, made sure to see Hyde Park, with its sidewalk speakers and its sometimes-harebrained offerings. The soapbox is a grand tradition that says ordinary people get a say. Free speech is protected. Audiences can be convinced. Words can change minds.

Our notions of what America stands for are bound up in the collective memories of speeches and grand outdoor events: the Lincoln-Douglas debates, John Kennedy's "Ask Not What Your Country Can Do for You" inaugural address, Martin Luther King's "I Have a Dream" speech, or George W. Bush's remarks from the wreckage of the World Trade Center. Every four years I religiously tune into the Democratic and Republican conventions to listen to the keynote addresses, to hear about the values that define our country, and understand how our leaders weave a narrative with personal stories and historic references. In 1984, New York Governor Mario Cuomo told the story of inequality by spinning a tale of two cities, one rich and one poor. Decades later, in 2004, Barack Obama spoiled us with his soaring rhetoric, lifting us up and making us believe that we were one country, not two divided into "red" and "blue." "Yes, we can," he said, and I believed him.

People say they hate speeches, but really, they listen, for better or worse. They respond to the vision, the values, and the intention. Later, they compare the words to the deeds and tune out when they don't match.

My fascination with political speeches didn't start with conventions and inaugurals, though. It came from an old family story about my great-grandfather, James H. Whitcraft. Whitcraft was a beloved schoolteacher and a proud

Civil War veteran who was active in almost every civic club in his hometown, especially the Democratic Party. In 1924, Whitcraft had a hand in organizing a huge campaign rally for local congressional candidates on the Chester County Courthouse steps. A crowd of nearly 1,000 assembled late on an October Saturday at the foot of the Soldiers and Sailors Monument, a huge bronze statue of a military man cloaked in Old Glory. It honored local soldiers who had fallen during the Civil War.

There were speeches. Candidates for Congress and the county commission gave their pitches. James Whitcraft and his grandson held their caps and coats as they mounted the platform to give their formal exhortations. Suddenly, there was a lull. One of the key speakers, Major John A. Farrell, had not appeared. He was on his way, they said, and would be there momentarily. To hold the crowd, my great-grandfather offered to say a few words about democracy. It was his favorite topic. His offer was accepted, and the old gentleman took the stage unprepared, but with no shortage of ideas about two champions of democracy—President Andrew Jackson and Henry Watterson, a former Tennessee congressman then the editor of the *Louisville Courier.*

Whitcraft was something of an amateur orator. Leafing through old papers, I have found weathered copies of speeches that he gave just to his family on occasions like his mother's 75th birthday, or his own golden wedding anniversary, which had been celebrated at a large party the previous year. All were flowery, religious, intellectual, and laden with historical references and quotations from "the classics."

I don't know why he chose to praise Andrew Jackson, the force behind the tragic Long March of Native Americans into the Western territories, as an exemplar of democracy.

Perhaps it was simply that Jackson was the first Democratic president. He certainly would not have been my choice. Yes, Jackson was a populist—the first Westerner in the White House and the champion of the "common man"—but the common men he championed were white, pro-slavery, and violent. Anyway, the question is academic.

Before Whitcraft had finished ad-libbing, he hesitated, suddenly pale, and fell backward on the platform. The crowd closed in. A doctor in attendance was summoned. He was carried to the green, grassy lawn surrounding the courthouse. His grandson, Alger, standing in the audience, didn't dally. He ran straight to the men's clothing store owned by his father, one block away, where he summoned his reluctant father, then waiting on a customer, to come quick. Granddad had collapsed while making a speech.

They needn't have rushed. James Whitcraft had fallen dead under the flag in front of hundreds of townsfolk, and their wives and children. According to the *Daily Local News,* a car was summoned, and James was taken to his home on South Church Street. No one could have revived him. It was a shock to the whole town.

I have tried to make sense of this story for years—to figure out whether it held any lessons for me as a public servant. What strikes me now is how different his audiences were from my own at the turn of the same century. The experts tell you every speech must be attuned to its particular audience, and his was clearly directed to that community's love of history, its old-fashioned patriotism, and its unquestioning belief that elections and democracy mattered. Here they all were assembled in front of the flag—women in frocks with dropped waistlines and men in the soft caps of the day. They came to hear the stump speeches from the men on their soapboxes. They were not cynical. They were engaged. They thought it all mattered.

The Republican Party won the elections again that year and Calvin Coolidge was elected—despite the Teapot Dome Scandal (with its New Mexico roots), which scarred the previous administration of President Warren G. Harding. The Democrats on the stump railed against the administration's rampant corruption to no avail. The Republicans carried Whitcraft's Pennsylvania as well as every state outside the South, except Wisconsin, which was won by Fighting Bob La Follette, a progressive.

My great-grandfather, I concluded, died filling in for someone else who did not appear. He picked up the slack, glad to do it for the greater good, for the Democratic Party, and for the awaiting community. His cause lost and perhaps he knew it would. Chester County was a heavily Republican area then and continued to be so up until Barack Obama carried it in 2008.

His speech was not just egotism or preening in public. It was public service, the kind that I wanted to offer, but with different values, different words, and a different audience. My job would be to address the spiral of cynicism, the apathy I found among my neighbors and friends, and the pessimism than ordinary people felt. Looking back at the speeches I gave to women's groups, for graduations, or at neighborhood gatherings, I try to remember what I was talking about.

Half of the time I was in cheerleader mode convincing citizens that they had political power if they chose to exercise it, to vote, and to make their voices heard in the halls of the state legislature, on the streets, or at the ballot box. I peppered my speeches, and later my books, with examples

of how one person can make a difference, even with few
resources or no connections. It used to be pretty standard
stuff. I included tales of cancer and AIDS patients who got
the legislature to pass a medical marijuana bill or the mother
of a teen who overdosed on opioids who started a treatment
facility for teens and got more funding for behavioral health.
I told of ordinary people with a big idea who were able to
get it adopted into law or who started an enterprise to do it
themselves.

My idea was, as Jesse Jackson had said in 1984, "to keep
hope alive" in a time when the faith that the townsfolk of
my grandfather's era had in their leaders, their government,
and their institutions was waning. It wasn't easy. The power of the 1% kept increasing and special interests began to
dominate elections with campaign contributions further
unrestrained by the US Supreme Court's Citizens United
decision in 2010. Health inequities, social inequality, and
the racial divide increased. No matter how eloquent you are,
the principle that one person has power is a hard sell with
gerrymandering, voter suppression, and crony capitalism all
on the rise.

I often ended my speeches with a line I heard somewhere,
"Don't give up and don't give in, in the face of disappointment and defeat. Your vote and your voice count more than
you think. No one makes a bigger mistake than those who do
nothing because they can only do a little."

Sometimes I could see it register. More often I felt a
flicker of recognition at the phrase "disappointment and
defeat"—something I knew all too well. I waged one losing campaign after another during the 1980s. My own 1995
campaign for the city council was a tremendous letdown
for all the supporters I had assembled. After knocking on

3000 doors, and losing twenty pounds, I lost by nine votes. It seemed like the end of the world.

The morning after I lost my 1995 campaign, I sat in my living room in my bathrobe, as one volunteer after another came by to urge a recount. People called on the phone to tell me how they hadn't made it to the polls because they had to take their mother to the hospital, or the dog had escaped and they were looking all over for it. It was a sad day. We took down all the signs, tossed out the walk lists and phone scripts. It took about a week. In the process, I drove by a sign posted on the marquee outside of Del Norte High School. It said, "The most important political office is that of private citizen." It was part of the "Character Counts" campaign fashionable in schools then. It applied to me and all the people who had participated in the campaign. I sent it as a thank you to my volunteers. The campaign had changed us, convinced us of the power of group action and the worth of belonging to something bigger, something based on shared ideals and common values. Politics, it turned out, was not just for candidates or politicians, but also for citizens who often become the builders of social movements.

I never thought I would run for office again, but the very next year, a rare open seat in the New Mexico Senate came up, and although I was exhausted, I decided to go for it again. Coming back from an initial failure—in a campaign, a soccer match, or from a fight for a cause that fell short of the goal—became a theme of my stump speeches. Who doesn't know the sting of defeat and disappointment? It's a common experience, especially for women running for office the first time or advocates trying to advance a big idea. Persistence was the point.

It wasn't just rhetoric. Once in the legislature, I felt the sting of defeat over and over. My big bills to get mega-money out of politics or provide universal healthcare at an affordable price almost always fell short. I didn't give up though, choosing to focus on incremental measures like requiring more transparency in campaign contributions, or more scrutiny of suddenly spiking health insurance rates. I took smaller bites of the apple and hoped that no one noticed that I'd just required insurance companies to cover cancer clinical trials, or a few extra days in the hospital for women who had just had a mastectomy. I was advancing the ball down the field, as far as I could. In the future, someone else would carry it farther. Maybe it would be someone listening to a speech.

Everyone needs a motto, a meme, or just a tune to play in the back of the mind when tackling a tough task like completing a degree, cleaning out the garage, or finishing a round of chemotherapy. My motto was developing a "passion for the possible." It was a phrase used by one of my heroes from the anti-war era, the Reverend William Sloan Coffin, the pastor of Riverside Church in New York City. I believed in the phrase for what it said about both idealism and pragmatism, and how both are key to political change and, on another level, living a fulfilled life. Now I had a chance to share the motto—and the philosophy.

And share I did. In 2012, I told UNM political science graduates they should develop that kind of passion and roll with the punches. "There will be punches; there will be losses," I told them. "There will be roadblocks and gridlock. But things change, the road opens up. History does not run in a straight line. There is no longer a straight and narrow path."

After the coronavirus and the ensuing recession hit New Mexico in March 2020, a straight and narrow path to progress became even more remote. Governor Michelle Lujan Grisham changed the tone of her upbeat speeches to meet the challenge. I had encouraged people in times of cynicism to keep the faith and believe that they had power. She asked even more. The Governor had to convince people to do things that they didn't want to do for the good of the whole. Like a good mother she repeated her points, clarified the data, simplified, and repeated again. Some constituents didn't like it. Then she had to justify punishment for those who refused to heed her warnings and comply with a shutdown—tough love. For the most part, it worked. New Mexico was rated highly among the states for its coronavirus response.

I was lucky I didn't have to force my listeners to do anything. On the senate floor or at rallies outside the capitol for bills to ban the death penalty, or to provide funding for people with mental illness, my job was only to persuade. I couldn't force anything. Usually data alone didn't do it. I made countless speeches about how secondhand smoke in restaurants and bars caused cancer, how wearing helmets when driving ATVs saved lives, or why banning fireworks in a time of drought made common sense. I was not getting the essential point. Values, especially when they are shared, and personal stories are far more important than facts.

Two ordinary citizens, Erin Armstrong and Essie DeBonet, had much more success in getting legislators to endorse marijuana reform than I did. Their stories of weight loss and pain evoked compassion, that greatest of all shared values, and it enabled senators to vote to legalize medical marijuana.

It was a point my great-grandfather knew implicitly. His last speech, according to the yellowed local newspaper I consulted, was composed of anecdotes about the "Torchbearers of Democracy."

I keep coming back to that speech, and to the theme of democracy. I didn't think about it much when I was a senator, but now I think it may have been what made me love public speaking, suspend my stage fright, and step boldly onto the platform. I never passed up the opportunity to speak and to share my values. While other legislators urged caution or ducked hostile audiences, I wanted to speak up. That was what I was there for, not just to get re-elected.

What was the worst that could happen? Well, I knew what the worst was. So, I'd better be prepared—with stories, surprises, or startling facts. I might never have the chance again.

16

Taking on the Big One

Summer 2009

I LOOKED OUT OVER THE HUGE CROWD ASSEMBLED that evening in the Plaza Mayor of the National Hispanic Cultural Center. I recognized some familiar faces. There was Mandy Pino from Health Action, Ted Cloak from Democracy for New Mexico, and some medical students from UNM. Organizing for America, a national group affiliated with the Obama campaign, had staged the rally, and a huge blue bus with a sign that said "Health Insurance Reform Now" was parked immediately behind the stage. It was on a cross-country trip, picking up doctors and people with pre-existing conditions with stories to tell along the way. Across the states, the effort to pass the Affordable Care Act was blowing up. The Tea Party was storming the Senate Office Building in Washington with signs depicting President Obama as a witch doctor from

Kenya with a bone in his nose. Rumors were spreading about death panels, rationing medical care, and creeping socialism.

Along with a dozen other state legislators who specialized in healthcare, I had been asked by the Obama White House to drum up support in my state, and to advise the President's staff on our experience with reforms already in motion out in the states.

Now, on a summer evening in 2009, the staff on the bus wanted to make sure I would stick to the talking points. I smiled. I knew what I wanted to say, and it was grounded in the local, not the national.

As I sat on the stage while others made their speeches, I looked more closely at the crowd. There was a contingent of doctors, some in scrubs, and some in white coats. I recognized the ones I had worked with on public health and prescription drug legislation. They knew what I would say. They knew the New Mexico status quo—the one in four New Mexicans without insurance, the crowded emergency rooms, the small businesses which could not afford to cover their employees, and the high rate of chronic disease.

When my turn came, I began my speech with a reference to another great one:

> 'The fierce urgency of now.' That's what
> Martin Luther King called it in 1967 at the
> Riverside Church in New York as he realized
> that unless civil rights advocates, students,
> and Americans from every race, creed, and
> ideology joined together, the Vietnam War
> would destroy the Great Society and divide
> and devastate a generation of idealistic young
> Americans.

It is a phrase that Senator Barack Obama used last year to inspire millions of young Americans to vote and to believe that they could change the future, even against insurmountable odds, vicious lies, and a racist rumor mill based on fears, not facts. And finally, finally, last week, we heard from our President. We heard that same focus on the moment, that same rejection of the status quo, and that sharp determination to act now.

The fierce urgency of now. Did you hear it? Did you feel it? Do you feel it now?

With their roars, the crowd let me know that they did.

I reminded them that the clock was ticking, the price of insurance was going up and that, as a result of a recession, there was no longer a safety net. I extolled the public option, and urged them to step up, to dispel the rumors of creeping socialism and government rationing and to contact Congress.

We must act now to build on our common values, our belief we are all in this together, and that, as our President said the other night, 'When fortune turns against one of us, others are there to lend a helping hand.' We must act now to say that...here in New Mexico hard work and responsibility should be rewarded with some measure of security and fair play and, yes, that sometimes government has to step in to help deliver on that promise.

Massachusetts US Senator Ted Kennedy was on my mind that night. He had died only months before, before he got a chance to see his lifelong dream of healthcare reform fulfilled. I had read his last letter to Obama on the subject and quoted it for the crowd.

I didn't think of it then, but the similarity of the speech to my great-grandfather's in 1924 is striking. A huge crowd. A podium full of speakers. A national issue. A Democratic issue. The opportunity to talk about heroes and values. James H. Whitcraft had picked Andrew Jackson and democracy. I chose Martin Luther King, Obama, and Kennedy. They were all Democrats, but that is where the resemblance ends. Although Jackson is credited with a popular revolt against a corrupt Eastern establishment, his Democratic Party was rural, pro-slavery, and anti-Indian. And Jackson was no Franklin Delano Roosevelt. Jackson wanted to weaken the federal government.

Democracy was to become an even more important theme for me as time went on, but in 2009, with the opportunity to enact the most far-reaching healthcare measure since Medicare was enacted in 1965, healthcare, for me, took center stage. It wasn't the first time I dove into this messy world.

~

Twelve years before, I had to make a key decision. Effective legislators specialize in a certain area. Education, criminal justice, taxes, the environment—they were all taken by ex-teachers, lawyers, business owners, or insurance agents. But there was one gaping hole—healthcare. No one seemed to have captured the field—for good reason. It was a tough subject that involved dozens of moving parts, all of them connected. There were medical questions, scope-of-practice issues, vested interests, public and private hospitals, insurance companies, nurses' unions, malpractice, Medicaid, and disability issues. Yet, it kept coming up at the door as I campaigned. People complained about Health Maintenance Organizations (HMOs), asked why they couldn't get a doctor's appointment, and had to wait so long in the emergency room.

I decided to take it on. I was not a professional. I didn't have a child with a disability or a serious medical condition myself, yet I knew that accidents could happen. I could sustain a traumatic head injury, menopause could throw me into a mental illness, or cancer could strike. I did get migraine headaches and the cost of medication was astronomical. I knew a little about Medicaid from my work with people with disabilities. The owner of a small public relations business, my own insurance premium was through the roof. I never tried to piece any of it together, though, or think about solutions.

The more I thought about it, the more fundamental it seemed. It was not just a technical issue, with medical solutions to scientific questions. Healthcare was a moral question that touched on justice and equality, two fundamental democratic values that have shaped American history. It's a sad reality that some of us are healthy and some of us are born with lifelong illness. It's unfair and unequal. Sickness could and does strike any one of us or any member of our family, at any moment. No one knows what will happen tomorrow. That's what binds us together in a web, into a community where we have an obligation and an opportunity to support one another. When we don't offer a helping hand—because it isn't the role of the government, or it costs too much, or it's a matter of personal responsibility—it's an indication of our character. Eleanor Roosevelt once said our national character will be judged, not by our economic prowess, but by how the weakest, the least among us, was treated. She was right. Going door-to-door, I had found out that ill health, sometimes a result of just the luck of the draw, led to a lifetime of poverty and lost opportunity. Without intervention, without a fix to level life's playing field in the right direction, this kind of healthcare inequity is the greatest form of social injustice.

So, I would begin. My mentor was an elderly gentleman from Las Cruces who, at the time, was the chairman of the interim Health and Human Services Committee, which became my home base in the legislature. Representative J. Paul Taylor was the kindest, most sympathetic person I ever knew. He wore his care for the poor, the abused, and the immigrant on his sleeve. He was known as the conscience of the legislature. Later, when I visited him at his historic home in Mesilla, I realized that the locals saw him as a saint. The local elementary school was named after him. There were scholarships, lectures, even special Masses in his name. People made way for him in restaurants.

When Representative Taylor left the legislature in 2005, he gave me a Nambe platter with the name of the Health and Human Services Committee engraved on it. He paid for it himself, since there was so little official recognition given by the legislature itself to the committee, which some called the "pain and misery" committee. I took it as a message to continue his work. I served as committee chair, alternating with a house member, off and on for over ten years, successfully sponsoring scores of bills on everything from organ donation to hospital report cards and suicide prevention hotlines. Committee meetings were long and intense. We heard personal stories from people with mental illness, the victims of elder abuse, pregnant teenagers, and nurses from hard-pressed clinics along the border with Mexico. We traveled around the state, took testimony from experts and citizens alike, and developed policy proposals to solve the problems we heard about. I learned everything I know about healthcare there. It was like taking three or four graduate-level courses—with practical applications—every year. Not everyone could bear it, but those who could—those who also bore witness to the needs expressed there—became my best friends in Santa Fe.

My first inkling that healthcare reform was possible came in 1998 when a group of doctors fed up with the first round of managed care—with its insurance restrictions, its gag orders on doctors, and its in-network-only referrals—joined forces with advocates for patients' rights. I signed up to help, to push a patient protection act through committees, and to learn the technical details of grievances and appeals to the insurance commissioner. I knew the people I met at the door during my campaign would be proud. They had regaled me with stories of how their new insurance companies would not let them see their regular doctor, or how their prescription drugs were no longer covered.

The Health and Human Services Committee led the way and with my fellow North Valley representative, Ed Sandoval, we pushed it through the legislature twice. It was finally signed in 1998. It was one of the first patient bills of rights in the country. The senior citizens advocates I had met and my constituents finally had a way to protest the injustices they told me about.

Two years later, after five attempts, we pushed through another "first"—a mental health parity bill that required insurance companies to recognize and cover mental illness as a biologically-based condition. We had finally overcome the opposition of the insurance companies with the help of courageous families who fought against the stigma of mental illness to tell us their stories. One of these families was the Domenicis, whose father, US Senator Pete Domenici, prevailed on reluctant Republicans to support the bill. People with mental illness had to wait eight more years until a parity bill, sponsored by Domenici and Senator Paul Wellstone, was enacted at the federal level. A true patient's bill of rights was finally incorporated into the Affordable Care Act in 2009.

Healthcare reform was beginning to seem possible. From the very start, I had told my constituents I was a reformer, and promised that I would keep chipping away, sometimes losing, sometimes winning.

Now came the chipping part. We knew that it would take a long time to get the big reform—universal healthcare coverage. A small band of us, advocates and reformers, kept at it—from both the inside and the outside. We knew we had to promote the ideas of transparency, competition, and the free market, not champion a government-run, single-payer approach to healthcare. I supported the idea, now called Medicare for All, but it had been defeated in the legislature year after year. Instead, to drive down prices for businesses and patients, why not assemble larger and larger pools of purchasers of insurance and prescription drugs? It was coming at the problem from a different direction. When going uphill, I figured, it's sometimes a good idea to approach from an angle, and change directions slightly, rather than plow ahead directly.

By 2009 I was regarded as somewhat of an expert on Medicaid, on prescription drugs, healthcare insurance, and public health. I joined with other progressive healthcare legislators at the National Conference of State Legislatures where we gathered momentum for some measures that later served as the building blocks for the Affordable Care Act (also called "Obamacare"). Then I was tapped by the White House to help pass and implement the Affordable Care Act from the ground up.

There was resistance from the usual suspects—the insurance and pharmaceutical companies and whatever allies they could muster to defend the status quo. Sometimes the resistance came from unexpected sources. The state's retirees, public school teachers, and state employees were satisfied with the insurance they received, even though the rising costs were outstripping their wages. A move to consolidate the groups, as other states were beginning to do, was a bridge too far. Not satisfied with letters and phone calls, people began appearing on my porch. They were retirees from the city or the county who would not even be included in any new purchasing pool, but the opponents had scared them to death.

This was not even a universal plan that included everyone, but it would have been a solid step forward. A year or so later, I helped the Richardson administration push for a true state plan—on the order of the one that had just been enacted in Massachusetts under Governor Mitt Romney.

The data was compelling. The studies we commissioned showed that the cost of doing nothing—of maintaining a status quo in which costs were skyrocketing and people were losing coverage every day—would be far greater in just two years than the cost of any state plan.

The data fell on deaf ears. A kind of trench warfare began, not between Democrats and Republicans, but between the Democratic leadership of the senate and the Governor. Senate President Pro Tem Tim Jennings and Senate Finance Chair John Arthur Smith thought that Governor Richardson was using the whole idea to run for president and make himself look better than the senate in the eyes of the public.

How dare he do this by actually trying to reduce the second highest number of people without insurance in the country! This was a federal matter, they said, best left to a new president. Even planning for a better system—using a healthcare authority, a consolation prize I had suggested—was defeated. By this time, I had learned it was wise to be there, Johnny-on-the-spot, with an alternative when the big initiative failed. It worked for me in 2007 when the senate spurned the ethics commission that I had long sought but felt pressure to do something—and that something was the public financing of state judicial races, which Representative Ben Lujan and I had been promoting. This time, however, I was caught in the crossfire. The administration didn't want a healthcare authority either, since it detracted from its larger plan, which was now dead as a doornail. Rancor had prevailed.

With the failure of a state insurance plan imprinted on my mind, I occupied myself with other programs—measures to shore up primary care in rural areas, to support promising new models of telemedicine and community health, and to provide free medical school tuition for at least one student who would commit to practicing primary care in rural New Mexico. In the following years I would pass incremental measures to allow 20-somethings to buy into their parent's insurance, transform the way we set health insurance rates, guarantee transparency, and curb denials. I would expand coverage for cancer clinical trials and human papillomavirus (HPV) testing and prevent higher premiums for women. Each bill was hard fought and each inch we gained was won with blood, sweat, and tears. It took a "passion for the possible," just like I had talked about in the campaign. I knew it was not enough, but the best I could do. Ultimately it paid off. Many of the reforms we enacted in New Mexico at that time were incorporated into the national Affordable Care Act. And they would be there, in state law, if the act was somehow repealed.

~

I was the final speaker at the Obamacare rally that evening. The deep purple clouds were moving quickly across the Sandias, to the east. It looked like rain. I closed the speech just in time with a reference to Ted Kennedy, the last of the Kennedy brothers. "The work goes on, the cause endures, the hope still lives and the dream shall never die," he had famously said. Healthcare reform was his lifelong dream, his passion, and now it was possible. With our help, Kennedy's healthcare dream, which had started with President Harry Truman, would become a reality.

As I wrapped up, a fine mist descended over the plaza, and people began climbing down from the wide concrete steps that line its south side. For the most part, the crowd stood still, even though it was beginning to rain. I thought they were sticking with me. But they saw something that I could not.

It was not a sudden collapse of a speaker, not the sudden death of a politician named James H. Whitcraft, who, in some parallel universe, had almost finished speaking and who happened to be my ancestor.

No—a huge rainbow had covered the sky behind me.

17

The People on the Porch

1997-2012

It's easy to romanticize the idea of representative democracy—hard-working elected officials carrying out the will of their constituents, solving problems, and coming up with policies that change the lives of millions for the better. The idea keeps you going from door-to-door, through rigged elections and strained relationships. What they don't tell you in New Mexico is that to fulfill that dream, you're on your own. Outside of the very short legislative sessions, legislators in New Mexico receive no salary and have no staff. They must rely on themselves to do the policy research, tend to their constituents' needs, and maintain their day jobs. It is what we idealistically call a "citizen legislature."

It takes a lot of work to maintain the romance.

About 50,000 people lived in Senate District 13 and over sixteen years it seemed like I had heard from most of them. I had gone door-to-door with notebook in hand asking people what their concerns were with state government, and now my constituents thought they knew me, from the fiesta at St. Therese, or our lunch at the Senior Center. Now that I was their senator, they expected service. Except for some angry cusses who just knew all politicians were crooks and blamed me for all the ills in the world, most still believed that politicians could solve problems.

I heard from them in meetings, phone calls, letters, and responses to my annual constituent survey. Sometimes it would be about a barking dog or a building down the street that was a monstrosity. Others were child custody problems. The caller always felt a tremendous injustice had been done. And they had already contacted lawyers, social workers, and tax advisors—I was their last hope. A grandfather on Beach Road in Duranes asked me to recommend parole for his grandson. He had fallen in with a bad crowd and become addicted to heroin, but he was a good kid. Countless parents were desperate to get their children into treatment programs—an almost impossible task after Governors Johnson and Martinez decimated and defunded treatment programs. They were counting on me for help.

For over sixteen years I kept every letter, answered my home phone without screening calls, and recorded every constituent concern in my constituent database. Every session I would bring back banker's boxes full of letters, and when I got home my inbox, a big blue ceramic bowl, was at least a foot and a half tall with more brochures, requests, invitations, and belated responses to my latest constituent survey. The next few months were devoted to filing, sometimes with the help of interns or volunteers. Most often I did it on my own. At the end of my time in the senate, I had stuffed eight filing cabinets, and filled even more shelves in the garage, where I rotated the files as they became dated.

One of these hundreds of callers, letter writers, petition signers, and appointment seekers was Bruce Canle.

To say that Bruce Canle was a regular caller is an understatement. Just when I would be leaving the house for an appointment, starting a speech for the League of Women Voters or a veterans group, there he was again, on the phone with a question about his benefits, a complaint about the lack of response from his congresswoman, or a story about how he was no longer at UNM. He called the house; he called my office in the senate; he called my cell phone. Once, he called on Christmas Eve, asking, "Is this a bad time?"

His problems had no easy solutions.

For years, Bruce Canle kept calling. He had an abscessed tooth, had gone to the emergency room, and waited there for over six hours for treatment. They told him he had to get to a dentist—quick. But finding a dentist was impossible. Bruce was on Medicaid, and, as I found out, only a third of all dentists even take Medicaid patients. There was a long waiting list.

He was already on the waiting list and had been for months. Once he'd made the bus trip down to a clinic in the South Valley but had been turned away at the end of the day. His landlord, Leon, who, I later found out, was letting him live rent-free in a little house off Rio Grande Boulevard, finally picked him up. The pain was excruciating.

I called the Dental Association. I called Community Dental on South Broadway. I called First Choice, a public health clinic that gave him an appointment—which he missed due to another emergency.

The next time he called, I think I was more distraught than he was. I was learning the failures of the dental system in New Mexico—the shortages, the prejudice against poor people who missed appointments, and against people with mental illness who were irresponsible. I learned employers were reluctant to hire someone with bad teeth.

This time, it was Bruce who calmed me down. He had a beautiful, gentle voice, and with it he told me his story. He was a musician in a band program at UNM. He played the trumpet. It was his only pleasure now that he was totally disabled by mental illness and on Social Security Disability Insurance (SSDI). With bad teeth he could no longer play.

Bruce put me in touch with his social worker. What? He had a social worker? I was glad to hear he had someone besides me, but where had she been? Finally, after a month or so, we got Bruce treated and on a plan to replace several of his teeth. His experience sent me on a six-year quest to increase the number of dentists in New Mexico and encourage treatment for people with disabilities. It's a systemic problem. New Mexico has no dental school. Our dentists are trained out of state and they tend to stay there. To increase the supply, we established a dental residency program at UNM, offered incentives to returning dentists, started pipeline programs to interest elementary students in the field, and provided more funding for dental education—with strings attached.

It seems obscure, but this is still a big problem in New Mexico. I think about it every time I go to the dentist. I've had the means to keep up my teeth. Most do not. You can tell by the periodic charity fairs where people line up for blocks to get their teeth pulled by dental volunteers, most often from out of state.

Now that I am out of office, I wonder what ever happened to Bruce Canle. Did he transfer his worries to another elected official? Or did he just want to talk to me. At the end he seemed to understand that I couldn't always help but I would listen and sympathize, no matter what. Often that was enough.

~

Another—even longer—quest than my dental adventure was spurred by a group of people who appeared on my porch one afternoon. They had called, and their problem seemed so overwhelming that I told them not to come while I thought about it. They came anyway, a mother and her daughter sitting on my porch swing while a young child played in the driveway among the wood chips. The mother said nothing as the daughter told the story.

Some months ago, her mother, an immigrant from Mexico, had become violently ill. No one knew what was wrong, so the family took her to the emergency room at UNM Hospital. They waited and waited. Finally, the mother was admitted. She needed an emergency operation. It was for some kind of cancer, esophageal, I believe. Upon release she needed chemotherapy treatments, which the family was able to pay for by selling some furniture and another child taking an extra job. But now the bill had come for the original operation, and the mother needed another. The cancer had progressed.

With their broken English and my limited Spanish, I could not get all the details. I did understand that they had no health insurance and the hospital had sent their bill to a collection agency, which kept calling and calling. The daughter had tried to negotiate with the hospital, but the discharge planners strongly encouraged the family to go back to Mexico where they said their mother could get the operation she needed for free, or at least for much less. "But how could she?" the daughter asked, reaching for her mother's hand. All the family was here and there was no one left in Mexico. And how could the daughter leave her children, her husband, and her job to go with her mother?

Just then the youngster playing in the driveway came over and climbed into his mother's lap. She rocked him in the old wooden swing we had hung from two old hooks. We never used it much, but now it was put to good use.

I thought of my grandmother, a Scottish immigrant, who had died years ago of breast cancer, surrounded by her family. Maybe this woman would not even get to do that. I could not hide my tears.

I could not solve that problem. I could only give them a drink of water. There were no easy solutions to the problem of the uninsured, immigrants, and people with low incomes. But now I knew the questions to ask hospital administrators and high-paid executives of HMOs: How many immigrants does UNM Hospital treat? Where does the funding come from? What are the legal requirements? What are the penalties for not following the requirements? What does the hospital do with its indigent fund and how much does it get from our property taxes? So many questions.

From my post in the senate, I could hold hearings, tell the stories I had heard, attract press coverage, and work with community organizations serving families like the one that appeared on my porch. I could identify points of leverage and work with others to demand that our public hospital, the one funded by our property tax dollars, provide indigent care to immigrants and others without insurance. It took many years, a slew of community organizations—Enlace, Pathways, Encuentro, Prosperity Works—plus intervention from Bernalillo County, before the hospital would change its policies.

Even now, the people on the porch still haunt me.

The drumbeat of personal problems brought to the doorstep of the local state senator—i.e., me—did not stop. Now, in the time of the coronavirus, it has intensified for elected officials of all stripes. Help with unemployment benefits, information about where to get tested, or where to get protective equipment may be a matter of life or death. Some elected officials are even doing the shopping for seniors or picking up prescriptions.

It seems selfish now, but at the time constituent problems drove me crazy. Foolishly, I thought my time would be better served studying the arcane details of healthcare financing, the reforms made by other states, or the best way to maximize federal funds for New Mexico. What I know now is that the problems brought to me by my constituents informed my policy choices. Not only that. The trust I saw people putting in me made me want to serve them, to listen to them, to prove that the government could help. Now, we hear so much about how public trust in institutions and politicians is at an all-time low. A spiral of cynicism—often deliberately cultivated—has taken hold. But it wasn't always like that and it doesn't have to be that way.

Public service is a two-way street. The more you listen to your constituents, the more you talk to them like adults, without slogans that simplify and divide, the more they believe you, and the more they become participants and partners—even when their problems have no easy solutions. Most elected officials know this, but then they think...*I have to get re-elected. I have to move up. I have to cover my flank.*

I learned that public service is more than making speeches—even if the speeches were to encourage civic engagement. It is also acts of kindness, the returned phone call, the little tweaks to make sure the tax refund is in the mail, and the condolence card sent when someone's husband has died. It is telling the truth.

The micro is the macro. I only realized this fully as I was leaving the senate. But it was not too late. Reading the paper one day, I saw the obituary of Aurora Zamora, a 77-year-old constituent I had met on the campaign trail. Politicians often give speeches about how this bill or that appropriations measure will affect the folks back home. They cite "Mrs. Murphy," or in New Mexico, "Mrs. Martinez," when warning of the effects of a property tax hike or a food tax. I had Aurora Zamora. I never mentioned her in speeches, but I thought of her once in a while in that vein.

I met her at her door on Sioux Avenue in Precinct 186 when I was first running for the senate in 1996. By all ostensible signs, she was poor. She loved her husband, Jimmy, who was ill at that moment, and she told me about her family and her life. She had eight children, seventeen grandchildren, and twenty-seven great grandchildren. She called me in 2004, one of the many seniors puzzled by Social Security, Medicare Part D, and other labyrinths without navigators or instructions. Later, I got her a $600 rebate through an obscure provision of the American Recovery and Reinvestment Act (ARRA), a stimulus program passed in the wake of the Great Recession. It was a small thing, but finally, I had made a tangible difference for someone who needed it. However,

Aurora—and other constituents—had given me much more by allowing me into their lives and showing me the personal side of the larger issues I was called upon to address.

18

The Hard Part

March 1, 2007

By 2007 I had been in the New Mexico Senate for a decade. I was in good standing with my constituents and in constant touch with them through my annual surveys. I had been re-elected twice. I had the best staff I could assemble for the Senate Public Affairs Committee, which I chaired. I knew all the players who appeared regularly to testify before committees. I knew the good guys from the bad. I had decided who to listen to and who to politely ignore. I had some triumphs—the Public Health Emergency Act, a safer system of driver's licenses for teens, helmets for young riders of all-terrain vehicles (ATVs), and insurance coverage for HPV vaccinations and cancer clinical trials. I was moving in the right direction.

Then came some tough times, both on the floor of the senate and then, the following year, in my own neighborhood.

~

There I was again. At ground zero, smack dab in the middle of the chamber—on the senate floor debating, answering questions, defending my bill, citing sources, fending off amendments from legislators looking to attach poison pills or to waste enough time to force an early adjournment without a vote. My reform-minded bills were always controversial, especially when they involved campaign financing or public access to senate proceedings. They took longer to pass through committees and always arrived on the floor near the end of the session. Time was never on my side.

This time, I thought I had a good chance. Senate Bill 800 was the capstone for a package of ethics reforms proposed by Governor Bill Richardson's task force in the wake of a scandal involving State Treasurer Robert Vigil. It would hold down the unrestrained flow of campaign cash to legislators from political action committees (PACs) and wealthy individuals to the limit allowed at the federal level. Most states limited contributions to far less.

I had been defending the bill for about two hours, rallying the Democrats to vote down one amendment after another—not an easy task, especially when there was only lukewarm support. Stuart Bluestone, from the Attorney General's Office was at my side, acting as an expert witness. Handsome, well-respected by legislators from his stint as a head bill drafter in the legislature, Stuart was my lucky charm and my assurance that nothing could go terribly wrong.

Most of the Democrats retreated to the senate lounge as Senator Rod Adair went into details of the constitution, Senator Bill Payne tried to "parse" the language, or Senator Stuart Ingle made bad jokes that everyone loved. They all had amendments. For each amendment, senators had to leave the TV, the ballgame, or come down from their offices to vote. This was not a process that increased the popularity of the pesky sponsor. If I hadn't had the support of Governor Richardson, the measure would have died long ago. There was only one final amendment suggested by Senator Lee Rawson. It was handwritten on the blue-bordered paper the senate uses for amendments.

When I read it, I had to sit down. I had mustered the energy to stand proud for over two hours, but now my knees began to buckle, and my legs gave way. I felt short of breath and my vision blurred. Stuart Bluestone, always composed, shook his head as he read the handwritten amendment.

It would have delayed the implementation of the bill until July 1, 3007—a full millennium later.

"It was just a simple amendment—only one digit was changed," Rawson said—and to my horror, it passed. The snickers and ridicule that came from throughout the chamber were aimed directly at me and my cause. I could have melted into the floor. This was a battle I had been fighting for ten years, as long as I had been in the senate, each year growing tired, gray, more wrinkled, and angry. I had invested so much in the effort—building alliances, trying to work with the Republicans, and learning the election code. It was all for naught. I had become a silly Doña Quixote tilting at windmills. My allies would surely see that I was not up to the job and move on to a more able sponsor next time. The Governor would forsake me. Perhaps I should just give up. Move on to easier bills. I took all this stuff too seriously anyway.

The senators didn't care about me; they were making a mockery of reform.

I had to beg Majority Leader Michael Sanchez, who hated the bill, to allow the amendment to be reconsidered, which he did. It was finally removed. The chamber stopped spinning momentarily. The bill then passed on to the house, where it passed quickly, with a few good amendments, but when it came back to the senate, it was killed in the final four minutes of the session. It lost by one vote.

The devastation was now complete. I had been worn down bit by bit.

About a week earlier in the session, I had been at the same spot, with a bill to open up legislative conference committees where the house and the senate hammered out their differences on the budget and other matters in secret. When the conference committees returned to the floor to make their reports, unexpected tax breaks or costly pet projects snuck through at the last minute. No one knew what had happened.

My expert witness, Bob Johnson, from the New Mexico Foundation for Open Government (NMFOG), which included several newspaper publishers, was barred from speaking by senate tradition even while he was viciously attacked by senators who had suffered unfavorable media coverage. A tax on newspapers was threatened. The revocation of non-profit status for advocates of the bill was mentioned. "How much are these foundation officials making each year, anyway?" one senator wondered out loud.

Bob Johnson, a tough former Marine and national Associated Press editor, did not suffer fools easily. It was all I could do to restrain him. His face was getting redder and redder, as the debate went on and on. He fidgeted in the chair brought by the Sargent of Arms. I feared for his blood pressure.

The Democratic leadership was particularly opposed. If we did this for the legislature, we should do it for the governor's cabinet meetings too, and maybe editorial boards should open their meetings, some said. The bill was an affront to the deliberative process and to the integrity of the senate. I was naïve, they said. I just didn't understand the need for privacy in forming policy. I had no sympathy for how difficult it would be to turn down supplicants publicly. The real decisions would be made outside of public view anyway, just like they always were. The senators all but patted me on the head and told me to go away like a misbehaving little girl.

I stood my ground for three and a half hours. I couldn't understand why the senate didn't see that their stubborn opposition made it look like they had something to hide.

There had been at least seven attempts to open up committee hearings since 1995. I had sponsored many of them. By the mid-2000s, forty states and the US Congress provided this kind of transparency. We now take it for granted—but not then. I had done everything right—formed a bipartisan coalition, which included not just the print media but the Albuquerque Chamber of Commerce, the Association of Commerce and Industry, and NMFOG. As a liberal Democrat, they were not my usual allies, but it takes a diverse community to build momentum, hang in there over the years, and finally pass lasting reform.

The bill was defeated, of course. When the vote was tallied (20 "no" to 19 "yes"), in a pure publicity stunt, I donned an old Red Cross scarf like nurses wore on the battlefield in World War I. Democracy had been severely wounded that day, I said, by backroom deals and secret meetings. Emergency rescue was needed. It was a cheap trick. What else could I do? I'd been banging my head against the wall for years on this—with no forward motion. What was I? An idiot?

The news media ran with the Red Cross story. It helped draw attention to the issue—for the next time.

By the end of the 2007 session, I had aged—without any of the benefits that age brings. My most important bill to limit campaign contributions had been lost by one vote to reversals and ridicule. It was defeated four minutes before *sine die*, the final motion to adjourn the session. I had spent the previous night on my couch in the office and I made it to my desk for the early morning start of the last, dizzying session with difficulty. Only coffee kept me going until my bill came up, and when it was defeated, everything went silent, even amid all the hubbub, the goodbyes, and the traditional "congratulations on a good session." All I could do was stare at the huge Seal of the State of New Mexico looming over the chamber. I knew the truth then—my entire time in this body had been pointless. I was like the ornate seal's dead snake about to be devoured by two powerful eagles. A familiar voice from inside my head arose amid all the chatter on the floor to say, "I told you so."

I wanted to flee the chamber and get back to my own office where I could safely break down. No such luck.

From somewhere toward the front of the chamber I heard my name called by Senator Pete Campos, who was presenting me with his traditional end-of-session Milagro Award for withstanding arduous debates and bringing forth cutting-edge legislation. I accepted the beautiful turquoise vase, with grace, but it was all I could do to suppress my outrage. Tears are rarely shed on the New Mexico Senate floor, and this time, mine seemed shed in gratitude, not anger. No one noticed the difference. I would like to have shattered the showy, expensive award right there, in front of the hundreds of staff, families, and lobbyists all crowding around for the traditional closing ceremony. It seemed like a consolation prize for my recent defeats. Yes, the large glass vase underscored the sense that you can fight tooth and nail, but you can never win—no matter how popular, or commonsense your reforms are, no matter how big the coalition you build, or how many facts you can muster.

I would always be the goody two shoes, the uppity woman, and the know-it-all. That seemed to be my fate.

Ethics Measures Sputter in Senate

Abq Journal 2/14

One Bill Advances, 10 Others Remain

By JEFF JONES
Journal Politics Writer

SANTA FE — A Senate committee's first crack at holding an "ethics day" to many of the ethics pending in the Rou turned out to be mos for reform advocate

A single bill that w corrupt state politi officials of their r pensions was advar Rules Committee but another measu expanding public elections stalled a to be in trouble.

The committe ended before 10 c bills on the agen discussed.

At least som unheard ethics be heard as early when the rules meets again.

The Rules Con first stop for ma ens of ethics bill in the Senate,

officials," said sponsor Sen. Sue Wilson Beffort, R-Sandia Park, whose measure now heads to the Senate Judiciary Committee.

expand voluntary

Ditch-to-Trail Bill

·EDITORIALS·

Ditch Users Must Unite

What a shame that three years of hard work on the Ditches With Trails project went down the drain at the Middle Rio Grande Conservancy District board meeting Monday night.

Thousands of people enjoy the shady, green ditchbanks that wander alongside the Rio Grande, whether they simply catch glimpses as they drive through the valley or actually take the time to walk a mile or two along a hidden ditchbank.

For years, word has been spreading from neighbor to neighbor that the irrigation ditches are a real asset to valley life, even if you don't own an apple orchard or alfalfa field. An entirely new group of ditch "users" has slowly developed — a recreational

...dents

to usable trails

last week that ity, and several ods will be bet-

y and irrigation they authorize used for trails stem or a trail t public entity. que, should be rough. She said en, we need the he trail will pro-

nservancy Dis- he North Valley

19

Trouble on the Home Front

March 2008

THE FIRST THING I DID EVERY YEAR AFTER the session adjourned in Santa Fe was to head for the irrigation ditch near my house for a long walk. Like so many Valley residents, I'm a dedicated ditch walker, devoted to those green ribbons of life, which irrigate farms, connect communities, and provide respite from the worries of urban—and in my case, legislative—life.

The first spring flows in the 300 miles of ditches criss-crossing the Valley are released by the Middle Rio Grande Conservancy District (MRGCD) around March 1st, marking the start of the irrigation season. By the time I reached them after the session's end, the ditches were full. Pairs of mallards and wood ducks were everywhere. People were out walking their dogs, taking photographs, posting flyers for lost cats, or taking a shortcut as I did so many times when campaigning door-to-door.

I was relieved to be home, and excited about the project that I had been working on for several years with the North Valley Coalition of Neighborhoods. It was coming to fruition. Now I had brought home the money to help the Conservancy District develop a better network of trails along the ditch banks. It was something I had been dreaming about for several years.

"Ditches with Trails" seemed like the perfect project for a public official like me. Here was a chance to protect a unique cultural feature that dated back to the original pueblos and formed the lifeblood of early Hispanic settlements. I could get behind a wildly popular project that had involved hundreds of citizens. There were working groups, Día del Rio events, ditch clean-ups, walk-to-school days, and guest speakers. There were lots of public partners—the city, the county, the Village of Los Ranchos, the National Park Service, the Open Space Division, the North Valley Coalition of Neighborhoods, Vecinos del Bosque (a South Valley neighborhood association), the Mid-Region Council of Government, and citizens of all stripes.

The problem was the MRGCD, a backwater of local government, which controlled the ditches and had erected "No Trespassing" signs on the ditch banks, which residents wanted to use for hiking, horseback riding, bike riding, or bird watching. Although subdivisions had long ago replaced fields, and most Valley property owners did not irrigate their yards with ditch water, they paid taxes to the District each year. Every year, I'd get questions from constituents. They wanted to know what they were getting for their tax dollars.

To encourage the District to shift its mission to include recreational services for urban dwellers as well as water for farmers in Socorro, Belen and other rural parts of the District, the project's steering committee worked successfully with Conservancy District staffers. The board voted to conduct a feasibility study and support pilot projects in both the North and South Valleys. They took a poll of ratepayers and found 83% were willing to dedicate a portion of their taxes to support a trail system. The MRGCD signed on and participated in community meetings and events.

~

The first hint of trouble came soon enough. It was a series of anonymous flyers distributed up and down Rio Grande Boulevard warning that a malicious group was seeking to pave the ditch banks and destroy the Valley's way of life. A new urban trail system, they said, would bring outsiders into private neighborhoods, create crime, spur vandalism, and disturb wildlife. Cars would flood neighborhoods as people from outside crowded in with their motorcycles and ATVs, looking for a place to park. Residents would be driven from their homes. Our agricultural heritage would be marred.

My email box started filling up with rumors about how I was trying to become the Queen of the Valley, controlling everything, wasting hundreds of thousands of dollars on a project that no one had been consulted about and no one wanted.

One flyer depicted a scene from the New York Marathon with throngs of runners crossing the Brooklyn Bridge, headed for the finish line, with a caption that said, "Expected by the Summer of 2010:The North Valley Welcomes the West Side."

Another was more personal. It said Senator Feldman is surrounded by lackeys and bureaucrats intent on destroying the American way of life. I was so controlling, apparently, that even my husband took orders.

It turned out that the source of the flyers was a man I will call Boyd DeLuca, the president of the Rio Grande Boulevard Neighborhood Association. It was a group that Mark and I had belonged to since the 1980s. In recent years, the once constructive group had descended into a not-in-my-back-yard, protect-my-property-at-all-costs organization headed by DeLuca. A small group of board members and other acolytes surrounded DeLuca, who had appeared suddenly on the North Valley scene. Any proposed change—zoning variances, new grocery stores, or improvements that might increase property taxes—were objects of its wrath. Board meetings were held in secret; elections were rigged, and the few members who could see what was happening felt like they were losing their minds and soon dropped out, leaving only the crazies.

A pedestrian bridge that had recently been constructed by Bernalillo County at the junction of the Griegos drain and the Griegos lateral (two different types of ditches) was a particular affront to the group. The bridge was not technically part of the Ditches with Trails project, but I had helped fund it with state capital outlay funds and hoped it would fit in with the larger project.

What really drove Boyd and his group berserk, though, was the fact that the bridge had artwork on it. It was absolute proof of an elite conspiracy to transform the rustic ditch banks into an urban playground, complete with concrete, steel and...ART.

Boyd and others on his board said the whole project had been concocted by bureaucrats, under cover, and sprung on the North Valley without public input or participation by neighborhood organizations. Trouble was, Boyd and some of his members had actually attended some of the scores of meetings that had occurred over the years, which they now denied had taken place at all. When this was pointed out, Boyd stopped coming to meetings...to strengthen his argument, I guess.

The vehement opposition came as a complete surprise. No real opposition had surfaced until the very last meetings, when Boyd had begun to beat his drum. Until then, the support seemed overwhelming. But somehow the screw had turned, and now I was the target of a smear campaign. Every time I went to the supermarket, I couldn't help but wonder if people thought I was a controlling, power-hungry bitch out to destroy the Valley. I wondered if that sidelong glance from Mrs. Contreras meant she knew. Or if those who had supported me would now turn their backs. I hadn't heard from Tomas Serna lately and maybe this was why.

Little did I know the worst was yet to come.

~

The Conservancy Board meeting to decide the future of the project was held on the second Monday in July in its nondescript, low-slung headquarters on Second St., south of El Modelo where everybody goes for tamales at Christmas. The monthly meetings were low profile affairs, but that night the crowd spilled out into the parking lot.

The stackable chairs were full of neighborhood folks, county planners, and horseback riders. One teacher had brought her class from Corrales. People clad in cowboy hats, jean jackets, and work boots lined the walls. The noise level rose as board members filtered into the room.

Finally, the chairman called the meeting to order, and announced its purpose. He was about to proceed to public testimony on Ditches with Trails, when someone suggested that it might be well to hear what the official plan actually proposed. Reluctantly he called Rebecca Alter, from the Bernalillo County Planning Department, to make her presentation. She was a few sentences in when people began to heckle her—yelling about the costly bridge that was put in without any input, laughing hysterically when she mentioned placing enlarged maps at locations along the ditch, so people knew where they were going. Every time she mentioned the words "trail network," the audience tried to shout her down. Some were singing the tune to Joni Mitchell's "They Paved Paradise and Put up a Parking Lot," with adapted lyrics courtesy of Boyd DeLuca's flyers.

About two hours of testimony ensued. Angry opponents spewed vitriol against the bureaucrats—the "planning class," they called them. They railed against outsiders who would block our driveways and overrun our neighborhoods if this project came to pass; against the effete cyclists and urban snobs who didn't understand the Valley's agricultural heritage. The pitchforks were up and the knives were out.

Passionate supporters of the project spoke about how they loved the rural feel of the ditch system and didn't want to change much, just enhance what we already had. Some spoke of ditches that had been lost—bought by property owners for development. Others were taxpayers who were sick of being ignored by the Conservancy in favor of farmers from Socorro. Children read poems.

I gave my formal remarks, recounting how the Conservancy District had been one of the originators of the project, shaping the feasibility report and signaling its support at every turn. I recalled how, when their board members had expressed concern about liability for accidents on the ditches due to increased recreation, I had solved the problem for them with a law I shepherded through the legislature.

I was eminently reasonable.

A long, icy silence greeted my remarks.

I don't remember whether Boyd DeLuca, whose lies had stirred up this opposition, testified himself. He didn't have to—he had the ear of one of the board members, Jim Roberts, who had done a U-turn on the project after (he said) receiving 400 letters in opposition. Roberts and another board member, Janet Jarrett from Valencia County, had a plan. Board Member Bill Turner, who had run against me in 1996 (losing by almost 70%), was along for the joyride.

The most moving moment of the night, I thought, was the testimony given by Lisa McKinney, a Lee Acres resident whose husband, a young emergency room doctor, had been killed while biking across a decrepit two plank bridge over the Griegos lateral a few years earlier. His bike slipped off one of the planks and although he was wearing a helmet it did not protect him when he struck his face, was knocked unconscious, fell into the water, and drowned. It was precisely where the new bridge had been constructed. Lisa McKinney had decided not to sue the District, hoping to put the tragedy behind her. Now, she simply wanted to testify in favor of the bridge and in support of the Ditches with Trails project.

Lisa had not quite taken her seat when she was sharply rebuked by Janet Jarrett. Jarrett wanted to know why Lisa thought her story, sad as it appeared, had any bearing on this discussion. It was no reason to erect a monstrosity or allow the takeover of the whole system.

It was then that I realized something abnormal, something sick, like a fever or a tide of anger and resentment, had taken hold.

Lisa McKinney began to cry. Jack Pickering, a 94-year-old neighbor I had brought to give the project an air of respectability, stood up and started booing the board, "Shame, shame, shame on you."

Jarrett was not deterred. Neither was Jim Roberts, who had a long tirade prepared for the occasion. This was a takeover by the "planner class," pure and simple. People were already using the ditch banks, and now a small group wanted to commercialize, urbanize, and desecrate the ditches with asphalt, steel, and concrete, he said. "We don't need any signs telling us a tree is a tree." The audience erupted into applause.

Roberts, of course, knew all about the feasibility study that the District had done and the poll it had conducted that showed support from 83% of its ratepayers. He had attended several community meetings where broad support for the project was clear. But that was then, and this was now. Here was the mob.

At the very lowest local level, he understood the iron laws of politics formulated by the late US Senator Everett Dirksen: "First law—get elected. Second law—get re-elected."

Bill Turner was working off another law of politics—demonize your opponent. I was that opponent—a power-hungry woman who knew no limits, who had abused her popularity, who was a media manipulator, and now was on her way to becoming a dictator. Pretty soon this machine politician, this hack, would be telling everyone what to do with their private property.

In the Conservancy's kangaroo court that night the rest of the board snapped to and unanimously voted for Jarrett's motion to end the Ditches with Trails project. A few weeks later, in a subsequent meeting, Jarrett and Roberts tried unsuccessfully to get the artwork stripped from the bridge crossing the ditch where Lisa McKinney's husband had died.

When I got out to the parking lot that night, I went numb. A friendly reporter who was just as shocked as I was walked me to my car. All I could do was mumble some incoherent nonsense about how change is difficult.

For months I mourned the District's abrupt turnabout. I had gotten behind the plow and pushed state funding into what I saw as a model project. I had been snookered into removing liability for their ditch-bank activities. But there was something more. How could the lies about me—about the project—have taken hold so easily? Would every cooperative effort be scuttled by anger and fear stoked by one disturbed individual?

Lies have a currency all of their own, just like Tom Udall had told me. Like money changing hands, falsehoods can travel far and wide before anyone discovers that they are counterfeit. In those days before social media, the flyer, the rumor, and the mob mentality were the coins of the realm. Soon thereafter we moved on—to the birther movement, based on lies spread by Donald Trump through right-wing talk show host Rush Limbaugh screaming that President

Barack Obama was not born here and was really a Muslim from Kenya. Later there was the idea spread by Steve Bannon of Breitbart News, another right-wing news outlet, that a hidden "deep state" was working secretly to undermine the will of the voters and elected officials. Obamacare, others said, would lead to death panels and socialized medicine. Just like Ditches with Trails was the first step in a government takeover that would destroy the way of life in the North Valley.

The incorrect information seems easy to spot. But it's one thing to know all this intellectually. It's another to be on the receiving end, wondering if it is your fate to keep denying the charges or whether you should simply resign yourself to the reality that some people will always think you are the devil incarnate, no matter the facts of the situation.

I know now that the sudden uprising against the Ditches with Trails project was Trumpism writ small. The Tea Party, which would surface a few years later, and other naysayers are more than willing to lie to prevent change. Private property owners have rights, and when they are threatened, even by as little as a trail nearby, they take out their anger on the government, its representatives (and senators), and those who dare to believe in a common good.

20

The Long Game

January 2009

ONCE I RETURNED TO SANTA FE THE NEXT YEAR, I focused on health insurance reforms and then, the new president's Affordable Care Act. I never gave up on my good government reforms though, and in 2009, the dam finally burst. My allies from the more liberal house had been steadfast in their support of campaign finance reform, ethics, and transparency, even while the senate and its Democratic leaders thumbed its nose at my measures. Ultimately, they forced the issue—and I was there to help.

Rep. Joe Cervantes, who is now a senator, carried the open conference committee bill I was so beaten up over two years earlier. I carried a duplicate bill that year, but it had been held up until the last minute—as usual—by the Senate Rules Committee, and its reform-averse chairman. I persuaded Majority Leader Michael Sanchez to hear Cervantes's bill instead of mine on the senate floor. He insisted that Sen.

Linda Lopez, the Senate Rules Committee Chair who had opposed the bill previously, have the honor of carrying it on the floor. The leadership, resentful that transparency could no longer be resisted, wanted to make sure I didn't get any credit for the bill I had carried for a decade. It was a slight, the kind of personality politics often played in the senate, but I didn't care. I remembered the old adage: "The progress you can make is in inverse proportion to the credit you want to take."

The bill passed this time with the help of several new liberal senators who had replaced the opponents of the open government measure. They were Tim Keller, Eric Griego, and Peter Wirth. The new team—particularly Senator Peter Wirth—helped get another of my long-sought bills over the finish line—the same one that some wanted delayed until the next millennium. Limits on campaign contributions finally passed in 2009. I had introduced my first bill in 1997, with the help of Attorney General Tom Udall. He was a great ally, but even the AG could not overcome entrenched opposition. It took a decade to do that, but finally, with reinforcements, public support and a bipartisan group of allies on both the inside and the outside, we crossed the finish line. With the recession looming, there wasn't much time for celebration that year, but I no longer felt so alone, so stranded on the road to reform.

It was a giant step forward, however the very next year we took two steps backward. I was crushed when the Supreme Court decided the Citizens United case in favor of allowing corporations and unions unlimited spending on campaigns through SuperPACs that often didn't even have to reveal their contributors. The limits on contributions from individuals and ordinary PACs were immediately undercut, and the reform I had fought for became far less powerful.

At least in New Mexico we were moving in the right direction, advancing the ball down the field toward the goal of reducing the influence of big money on elections, and a system akin to legalized bribery.

~

During the same session that my good government reforms finally came to fruition I joined with several Albuquerque senators who were equally outraged by the Conservancy District and its arrogant, rogue activities. I had been a victim of their board, but now I realized that there were other victims, and they were ready and willing to coalesce.

Three bills were introduced in the legislature in 2009 to limit the Conservancy District's power. My bill, which received the most publicity, removed the District's tax revenue collected from Bernalillo County and placed it in a trails authority to be run by the Middle Rio Grande Council of Governments. Another bill eliminated the District altogether. The bills went nowhere, but they sent a message, and it was not just from one senator who had been cast as an enemy of the District, but from others who represented Valley areas.

The bills' message was received by two candidates who emerged to challenge trail opponents Jim Roberts and Bill Turner in the upcoming Conservancy District elections, a notoriously low-turnout, off-season affair, open only to property owners within the Valley.

Karen Dunning was a former neighborhood planner from the North Valley and Adrian Oglesby was an environmental advocate and water lawyer who had run for a spot on the

Conservancy District's board once before. Now they ran as a team for the two Bernalillo County seats on the board. I helped them by setting up phone banks, mailings, and fundraising. The Ditches with Trails constituency came through, propelling them to victory. Elections were something I knew about. As the results came in, we celebrated their victory in the same room where Ditches with Trails had been cast aside.

It was a new day for the Conservancy District. In coming elections more reformers would be elected—and they were not just ditch enthusiasts. They were water and public land experts. John Kelly, elected in 2011, had been the chief engineer at a sister agency, the Albuquerque Metropolitan Arroyo Flood Control Authority (AMAFCA), and his expertise added to Oglesby's. Joaquin Baca, a hydrologist with the US Fish and Wildlife Service, was elected in the next round, and in 2019 a champion of the Ditches with Trails effort, Barbara Baca, won the at-large position. Baca is a former planner with expertise in trail management.

~

It had taken twelve years, but we had completely reformed the Conservancy District. It will no longer be an institution mired in the nineteenth century, looking out only for a narrow—and shrinking—constituency of irrigators. Its controversial chief engineer, Subhas Shah, who at the height of his power was making twice more in salary and benefits than the Governor of New Mexico, is gone. Mike Hamman, a well-respected and more accommodating water resources expert, has taken his place.

Along the way, we modernized Conservancy elections, which were archaic. Only property owners were allowed to vote, with strict identification procedures. The turnout was not even 1% of eligible voters because the elections were held during non-election years in June. Even if you wanted to vote it was difficult. If you had to vote absentee, for instance, you had to have your ballot notarized—at your own expense. Voting machines rejected by the state (in favor of more secure paper ballots) were used in District elections to the dismay of voting-rights advocates.

Now, attempts at voter suppression in Wisconsin, Georgia, Florida, and other states have become commonplace and huge efforts have been mounted by Georgia voting-rights advocate Stacey Abrams, who narrowly lost her race for governor there in 2018, and others to fight suppression. But then the issue was not well defined. A few, like then Bernalillo County Clerk and now Secretary of State Maggie Toulouse Oliver, realized that the District's elections were the most restrictive in the state. Finally, they became the subject of an electoral reform task force, created by a measure I sponsored in the legislature.

The task force recommended eliminating notarized ballots (which the District finally did, but only after an AG's opinion) and combining the District's election with other small elections for school board and municipal positions. The combination would increase voter turnout in all the local elections. The Conservancy District resisted, of course, because for them increased turnout was a threat, not an opportunity. Nevertheless, an elections reform bill, passed in 2018, required the eventual consolidation of local elections. The Conservancy District maneuvered to be among the last to be included.

~

Every day since the start of the COVID-19 crisis, as I have been writing this memoir, I walk along the ditch near my house, which runs between Matthew Avenue to the north and Indian School Road to the south. I remember the angst that the Ditches with Trails project caused, the pitchforks, the angry meeting, and the neighborhood association gone awry. It seems like eons ago. But elections have had their consequences. After twelve years, a new version of Ditches with Trails is gradually coming to pass. The city, county, and Conservancy District have embarked on a multi-year, $15 million trail and ditch improvement project—tackling first the stretch along the Alameda Drain beside 2nd Street, extending along Matthew Avenue, and then on to I-40—right where I walk. The project includes paved bicycle paths, dirt walking areas, landscaping, signage, and...(gasp) sculpture.

I am finally experiencing the fruits of my labors. I know now, it's part of the long game—the permanent campaign. Progress made today is built on a foundation laid by others. Today's successes can be reversed next year, just as my campaign contribution bill had suffered a setback. But it's harder to bend the arc of progress back. Others will pick up the torch, stronger coalitions will form, and new laws will consolidate past gains. With a little kick, the ball will keep rolling.

21

The Tentacles of Corruption

March 28, 2019

A HIGHLY POLISHED TRAVERTINE TABLE forms the centerpiece of the New Mexico Governor's office on the top floor of the Capitol in Santa Fe. It is so big that it fills an entire room. Its radiating bands of tan, cream, and brown point to the edges of the round table, where scores of reporters, state police, teachers, judges, legislators, businesspeople, film stars, and even foreign dignitaries have been seated for ceremonial occasions.

Travertine, formed when groundwater infused with calcium carbonate (usually from ancient hot springs) percolates through limestone, is native to New Mexico. It is underfoot on floors and stairways throughout the Roundhouse. And the cool, striped stone from quarries outside of Belen, New Mexico, lines the walls and forms the rotunda at the center of the unique building, which is laid out in the form of a traditional Native American symbol. Travertine is now commonly used for tiles and fountains, but a seventeen-foot-diameter travertine table is rare.

A few years ago, on March 28, 2019, I found myself sitting around the huge table, running my fingers across its smooth surface, admiring the complex Zia sun symbol in the center. The table had been a familiar fixture for me during the Richardson administration, and it was there, under the Great Seal of the State of New Mexico, that I received the red pens used by the Governor during signing ceremonies for bills that I had passed. Seated around the table this time, elbow-to-elbow, were my fellow good government advocates from Common Cause and the League of Women Voters, a slew of reporters, Governor Michelle Lujan Grisham, and a new set of Democratic leaders.

The New Mexico Ethics Commission was about to become law.

The sponsors of the long-delayed bill, Senator Mimi Stewart and Representative Daymon Ely were jubilant. But no one was more jubilant than I was. There had been over 50 bills to establish a commission during my time in the legislature. I had sponsored many of them. They all had foundered in the senate. What I had failed to accomplish in my decades of work from the inside, I now accomplished from the outside, working with an inveterate group of reformers and activists, many of whom I knew from my time as a senator.

Even before I was elected in 1996, I had promised that I would be a reformer working to ensure that each person's vote counted equally and the law-making process was fair and transparent, particularly when it came to the way our elections were financed. I introduced at least one measure every session to limit the influence of special interests and big money. The bills were a tough sell, but I hung on until I passed some to limit political contributions, institute public financing for some races, and make campaign reports public on the secretary of state's website.

When I left the legislature, however, there was one major piece of unfinished business. New Mexico was one of only eight states that did not have an independent ethics commission to hold government officials, candidates, lobbyists, and contractors accountable when they violated the law. The measure had huge public support (over 80% according to several Common Cause polls) but I was never able to overcome entrenched resistance from the senate leadership, which was offended at the very idea of oversight from anyone outside of the institution. It was one of my deepest regrets when I left the senate, and I felt ashamed for our state as we endured one scandal after another. Public trust that wrongdoers would be held to account was taking a beating, and the state's national reputation plummeted.

~

It had been seven years since I left the legislature, wondering how I would continue my life without immediate access to power. Would anyone hire me? Could I go back to freelance journalism? My husband was happy to have me back home, but I was adrift. Then, I got lucky. Common Cause, the good-government group started by President Lyndon Johnson's Health, Education and Welfare Secretary John Gardner in 1970, came knocking. They weren't the giant health care conglomerate or the prestigious public institution where I had fantasized that a job awaited. They were better.

Fifty years ago, they recognized the key political issue of our times—corruption—and the key remedy—democracy. Business has been brisk since Donald Trump was elected president in 2016, bringing with him a tide of ethical violations, administration indictments, pardons for cronies, and threats of imprisonment for opponents. The once small but influential non-profit has swelled to over a million members—all of them eager to defend democracy and the rule of law.

It used to be that concerns about democracy rarely animated voters. But as news stories documented a new abuse of power every day during his administration, people began paying attention. The blatant promotion of Trump properties was hard to hide, even when the President has refused to release his tax returns. *The New York Times* documented sixty customers with interests at stake before the administration who spent nearly $12 million at Trump's golf courses and hotels. His use of government grounds to hold campaign events and government agencies like the Post Office to pursue partisan ends is well known.

As soon as Trump was elected, I began to keep a list of his lies posted on my closet door. After only six months, the list had exceeded the height of the door. My desire to scream had subsided, but I was only beginning to learn how to deal with the rage I felt as our system crumbled before my eyes. I am still dealing with it.

I am not alone. Groups I never knew existed are filling my inbox with calls to action: Fair Vote, Retake Our Democracy, Demos, Represent Us, and Public Citizen.

Opinion pages and blogs filled with columns by political scientists and historians who explained that these abuses were not technicalities. People ordered Sinclair Lewis's 1938 novel about fascism in the United States, *It Can't Happen Here*. They googled words like "oligarchy" and "plutocracy." They faced the reality of an executive who ordered the military to put down protest. They got a glimpse of what life without democracy might look like.

It used to be that only car mechanics knew what went on under the hood. Only the technicians noticed when the level of the car's brake fluid was low. Now the drivers have begun to ask more questions lest they become victims when the brakes fail. When a president and a political party are willing to scapegoat immigrants, suppress votes, toss oversight out the window, pardon cronies, and seek the assistance of autocrats instead of civil servants, the brakes are failing. Democracy is hanging by a thread.

Without it, corruption goes unpunished, authoritarian control flourishes, and there can be no reform, no change for the better. You can't have environmental justice, fair courts, or healthcare for all when you have an electoral system where election results can be overturned by the president or where money and special interests control the outcome. Heck, you can't even have accurate census data or unaltered weather reports. Without these things, the conversation is over. It is only about power and retaining control through whatever means possible. The rule of law, truth, compassion, and consistency don't matter.

Do I sound like a little old lady in tennis shoes? A civics teacher? Perhaps you think I am veering into the academic world of political theory. I claim rights. I am no stranger to corruption.

In the New Mexico Senate I sat in the third row from the front. For many of those years I sat next to Senator Phil Griego, a fellow Democrat, but my polar opposite. He represented Santa Fe and rural areas surrounding it. In real life he was the owner of a title insurance company and a licensed realtor. He took every opportunity to enrich himself, justified entirely by our unique "citizen legislature," which allows members to keep their businesses, introduce laws that favor their own interests, and live life large off the lobbyists who surround them, proffering dinner and a show at Vanessie, or a catered lunch from The Shed. I was alerted to Phil early on when he introduced a bill that would relieve title companies of any liability should the property titles, which they insured, be found faulty. *Hmm,* I wondered, *what do the fees we pay at closing for title insurance go for then?* But that was when I was young and naïve.

Phil has since served time in prison, but he was a powerful star in the senate while he was the chairman of the Corporations Committee. In a narrowly divided chamber, he was strategically located in the middle of the road between the Democrats and the Republicans. His vote could make the difference between victory and defeat if you wanted to increase tobacco taxes, ban cockfighting, or replace the death penalty with life without parole.

Yet Phil was not all bad. No one is. His brother died of AIDS. He struggled with alcoholism. He wanted to protect a rural way of life. Like so many people caught in a flawed system, Phil's corruption crept up on him. His best friends were lobbyists and his privilege crowded out everything else. Finally, he crossed the line. He pressured the legislature to sell a state building near the Roundhouse to a client and collected a $50,000 real estate commission for his efforts—efforts that only a legislator could have made.

A year or so after I left, he resigned, after putting his fellow senators in the awkward position of either condoning his actions, censoring, or expelling him. After that, he was indicted, convicted, and sent to the Central New Mexico Correctional Facility, where he spent a few years in prison, sick and disgraced.

Phil was one of three of my colleagues to spend time in the slammer. Senator Dianna Duran, who left the senate and became the secretary of state in 2011, was convicted of embezzlement for using campaign contributions to fund her gambling addiction. Ironically, the secretary of state is the state's top election official who oversees campaign finance reporting. And then there was former Senate President Pro Tem Manny Aragon. Aragon had upended the democratic process in the senate and cut corners in order to pass landmark legislation. Ultimately, that was not what did him in. It was sheer graft. In 2008, even as the senate was debating an ethics commission, he was sentenced to three and half years in a federal prison. His crime was siphoning off $600,000 from over $4 million he had helped the legislature appropriate for a new Metropolitan Courthouse in Albuquerque.

While I was in the senate, corruption was right next door and sometimes only a few seats away. It was not as overt as Donald Trump's behavior. No one can top him. Yet all the same hallmarks were there—the use of public office for private gain with justifications based on the need to maintain power to do a job, to help the "people," the party, or constituents. The result was the same—erosion of public trust and a kick in democracy's teeth.

In New Mexico, as one scandal overtook the next, a band of reformers—insiders and outsiders—pushed for an ethics commission to handle public complaints and hold public officials, contractors, and lobbyists accountable. They pressured the senate to address campaign finance violations, contributions given to officials in return for juicy state contracts, gifts given to legislators, and the failure of lobbyists to report money spent to wine and dine legislators. Their efforts were not successful. Bills were introduced. The House of Representatives stayed up all night working on them. Task forces came and went. Nothing ever came out of the senate.

A new approach was clearly needed. Now on the outside, I saw things with fresh eyes, and so did my allies—not just my old friends in Common Cause, NMFOG, and the Attorney General's Office, but a new group of advocates from the private sector, including the Albuquerque Chamber of Commerce, New Mexico First, and the NM Association of Commerce and Industry.

After banging my head against the senate's stone walls for years, I realized I could apply what I had learned from my trials and tribulations with the Middle Rio Grande Conservancy District. When you can't win on one playing field, it's best to shift to another. In the Conservancy's case it was switching to electioneering—electing new board members who were more responsive to the need for recreation and trails along the irrigation ditches. When it came to an ethics commission, it was taking it to the voters instead of their representatives.

Citizens don't have much opportunity in New Mexico to make their voices known directly. Yes, they can elect representatives, but in New Mexico there are no direct initiatives at the state level, where citizens can ratify propositions or other measures put before them. There is one exception, though, and we aimed to use it.

Constitutional amendments go to the voters once the wording has been approved by the legislature. That's no easy task, given that, to get on the ballot, amendments require an extraordinary majority of each house. Yet sometimes legislators are more willing to punt to the people in this way rather than pass controversial measures themselves. And, if the measure passes at the ballot box, they get to enact the details in "enabling legislation" during the following session.

It was worth a shot, given that the coalition had expanded beyond just the usual good-government suspects and we knew from polling data that we had the public behind us. It took several years, but with the absence of one of the senate's strongest opponents, Senator Michael Sanchez, who had been defeated in 2016, the resolution putting an ethics commission on the ballot was approved in 2017.

By that time New Mexico was one of only six states without a commission—but not for long. The next year, after an organized campaign led by Common Cause, the voters overwhelmingly approved a constitutional amendment creating a new seven-member commission. Now the communications director for Common Cause, I had enlisted former Governor Garrey Carruthers and US Senator Jeff Bingaman to the cause, written op-ed after op-ed, and then—at the last minute—held my breath.

I was overjoyed by the results—over 70% voted in favor of the commission. I celebrated over the phone with my old pal, Stuart Bluestone, who had retired from the Attorney General's Office. He had been in the trenches with me, testified endlessly, and sat on the floor as we defended accountability and confronted corruption. Our work was not done. We feared that the legislature would make the new commission into a toothless tiger by restricting its jurisdiction and shrouding its decisions in secrecy. During the 2019 session, there was wrangling over every detail. The Common Cause lobbyists worked overtime. Stuart Bluestone wrote letters to the Speaker. I wrote releases, tweeted, and Facebooked, following every detail from the outside. We wondered if the legislature would simply disregard the public and the bill would fail without even a vote. Finally, the senate acted, passing a last-minute, much-amended bill on March 13. The house followed two days later. There was not one vote against it in either chamber. Public pressure had done its job and the legislators rose to the occasion. The bill was signed by the Governor on March 28.

It had taken decades.

For years I had a 2008 cartoon drawn by John Trever from the *Albuquerque Journal* hanging in my home office. It was an aerial sketch of the Santa Fe Roundhouse (the state capitol) as a maze, with a Democratic donkey and a Republican elephant guarding the front door. The two of them were cheerfully admonishing a voter trying to gain entry not to worry. "Good news!" they said, "Ethics reform is just around the corner!"

The cartoon was finally out of date.

After years of attempts to untangle the tentacles of corruption and scores of failed bills, the NM Ethics Commission held its first meeting in 2019. Stuart Bluestone, my old ally, was among its members.

Epilogue

A DIVIDING LINE RUNS THROUGH all of our lives separating the time before the coronavirus and after. I wrote this memoir after that line was drawn in March 2020 during the year of the pandemic. During the last months of 2020, I thought I had finished just in time to turn the corner into a new era. A new president had been elected. A vaccine was finally on the horizon. I hoped life would return to normal. But that was not to be.

COVID-19 cases spiked, new variants arose, and Donald Trump hung on, insisting he had won by a landslide, that it was only the media, the voting machines, or the crooked election officials that kept him from his rightful place at the White House.

There would be no respite from disease—either physical or political.

~

For almost a year we have learned to keep our distance, our bodies separated from the others we encountered in the street, in the parking lot of the supermarket, or at the polling place. A masked woman, I have walked the ditches and the streets of the North Valley, stepping aside, letting others pass, making apologetic eye contact, waving in recognition on the path sometimes, shuddering as the unmasked jogger ran too close, yelled too loud, or breathed too heavily as he passed.

All along I pined for the days I talked to strangers in their doorways on Headingly Avenue or La Luz Drive, bought cupcakes at the bake sales in front of the John Brooks Super Market on Candelaria, or bumped into a friend at the Flying Star on Rio Grande Blvd. I am still hungry to hear their stories, even their complaints about property taxes or the "No Right Turn on Red" sign at the corner.

Now the things that brought us together—the handshake upon meeting, the raucous laughter, the hymn, the fight song, the hug to console after a loss—are still dangerous.

As the virus hung on and the political acrimony grew in the aftermath of the election, the longing for normality has only increased. We continue to fall off the cliff, with miles to go before we hit bottom. Along that downward spiral we have witnessed a violent insurrection to overturn the election on January 6, 2021, another impeachment, and a Senate trial. The death toll from the virus continues to mount, now far exceeding half a million Americans, over 4000 of them New Mexicans.

Still, during this purgatory, there have been brief moments of joy.

The Saturday after November's election my daughter, Abby, called from Durango. She knew about my phone calls to voters in Pennsylvania and Arizona; she knew about the bottle of champagne I had chilled in the fridge for a victory party, and knew that it remained there, as I anxiously awaited the final results.

She was jubilant. "He won! He won!" she yelled as the TV blared in the background. The absentee votes had come in from Pennsylvania, where I had grown up, and they had thrown former Vice President Joe Biden, the Democratic candidate, over the top. The TV networks called the election for Biden.

I cracked open the champagne and tuned in to the TV that I had turned off in frustration the night before. I could see Biden supporters partying in the street near City Hall in Philadelphia with its statue of William Penn. That afternoon, music was blaring, horns were honking, and people were literally jumping up and down, banging on pots and pans, and waving flags in cities from Chicago to Seattle. In a few hours, a spontaneous parade of celebrants also took shape along Central Avenue in Albuquerque.

The jubilation was caught on a video from downtown Albuquerque as a 26-year-old Native American man spontaneously jumped out of his pick-up and broke out into a traditional dance in the middle of Central Avenue. The video went viral, garnering over five million views on Twitter. Ashkia Randy Trujillo, of Tewa and Navajo descent, stomped and moved his arms like wings, telling a story of joy and endurance that captured my heart.

Later, responding to his newfound fame, he said, "To rejoice is to feel the pep in your step, the warmth in a laugh, the beauty of your smile, and the togetherness we share as one people looking for hope when there is none. That's the feel of rejoice that I shared with you all tonight."

We had survived. We were still alive in spite of the random killing of half a million of our people, the loss of jobs, the loss of security, and the loss of the company of our neighbors, our friends, and family. Joe Biden had won. Democracy had held—if only barely. Citizens had shown up to vote and overcame one barrier after another. The election officials would soon stand up for an accurate—and not a fabricated—vote count, and the courts soon would uphold the rule of law, reject conspiracy theories and brazen attempts to have the results overturned based on lies about voter fraud.

Yet in the election's immediate aftermath, there was a deafening silence from the White House, broken only by defiant declarations that the president had won in a landslide. There would be no concession speech, only repeated claims that absentee ballots were fraudulent, state officials crooked, and the election stolen.

For weeks after the election, leaders of the Republican Party refused to challenge Trump's unsubstantiated claims and accept reality. As lawsuit after lawsuit failed, and the intimidation of election officials commenced, Republican senators stood silent. They thought only of their base of true believers. Their emperor no longer had clothes. He had lost the election. Yet the courtiers still swarmed and the ministers still followed, admiring the fabric, touching the velvet, and asking to embrace the hem of his cloak.

In the next month, after last-ditch efforts to encourage legislators in Michigan and Pennsylvania to send their own slate of electors to Congress failed, and a frantic phone call to the Georgia secretary of state to find 11,780 votes was re-buffed, Trump turned to his supporters to "stop the steal."

The result was the storming of the Capitol on the day results were to be certified, January 6, 2021. The insurrection was televised live, and the images are now a part of history: the noose prepared for Vice President Mike Pence; the Speaker being rushed from the chambers; senators hiding under their desks.; the outgoing president urging the crowd to march down Pennsylvania Avenue; the Confederate flags, and the signs left behind saying "Murder the Media."

In hindsight it was all so predictable. After years of propaganda against enemies of the people, the deep state, the immigrants, the "nasty women," and those who wore masks, the conspiracy theories were believed. The evidence no longer mattered. The virus was a hoax, the Democrats were pedophiles, and billionaire George Soros had rigged the Dominion voting machines.

Still wearing my mask, I took to the ditch to ponder whether we could ever overcome the deepening divide. The rule of law and agreement on a fair process used to keep us on the same playing field. And belief in a baseline reality kept us on the same page. But now—in spite of the election of a more "normal" president—we are in uncharted waters. On some days it seems like civil war between the masked and the unmasked—between the red states and the blue—is inevitable. Since the election, Republican state legislatures in states that went for Biden have introduced over 250 bills to make it more difficult to vote. They want absentee and early voting limited, additional identification required, and ballot drop boxes removed. Sunday voting was to be curtailed in Georgia to prevent churches from busing their congregants to the polls. It is hard to not see the ghosts of literacy tests, poll taxes, and Jim Crow.

On the other hand, sometimes hope makes an unexpected appearance—in a women's book club jumping in to handle vaccinations in Silver City, New Mexico, or in the nomination of new US Secretary of the Interior Deb Haaland, a Native American woman from my New Mexico neighborhood.

Still, coronavirus and the election season have left post traumatic stress disorder in its wake. We don't yet know how long it will take for a sense of community to return. Will our fear of other people as dangerous—as potential disease carriers—last longer than we want? Will we further withdraw into ourselves, our houses, our own worlds of selected media, and separate political beliefs? Where will we find the surprises and the sense of connection I discovered behind all those doors I knocked on for over 25 years?

~

Meanwhile, the story I told in the preceding chapters doesn't really end where I've left it.

- The number of women in the New Mexico Legislature has hit a historic high at 37 in the house and 11 in the senate. Two of the senators, Brenda McKenna and Shannon Pinto, are Native American women. Three others, Liz Steffanics and Mimi Stewart in the senate, and Marion Matthews in the house, are veterans of early 1990s campaigns to elect more women in the aftermath of Anita Hill's testimony before the US Senate's Judiciary Committee.

- In March 2021, the New Mexico Environment Department sued Los Alamos National Labs over its radioactive waste disposal practices, a topic I wrote about in 1979.
- Ward 11A, once chaired by Tom Castillo in Albuquerque's North Valley, has become one of the most active Democratic wards in the city, spurring increased voter turnout and participation at forums, rallies, and conventions.
- The Middle Rio Grande Conservancy District has partnered with the city and county on a $15 million project to improve ditch banks and drains in the Albuquerque area, essentially implementing the Ditches with Trails initiative.
- Healthcare reform has continued with new legislative champions—Representatives Debbie Armstrong, Liz Thompson, and Senator Jerry Ortiz y Pino.
- Transparency has emerged as a common value between Democrats and Republicans in the legislature with more public meetings and documents.
- Governor Michelle Lujan Grisham continues to hold weekly news conferences on COVID-19, using her bully pulpit to urge social distancing and mask wearing. The state's vaccination rate is first in the nation.
- The bipartisan New Mexico Ethics Commission began taking complaints and issuing opinions about violations of campaign, governmental conduct, procurement, and lobbyist laws in 2020.
- Campaign contributions and spending in New Mexico continue to escalate, with more and more PAC money coming from outside the state. In 2020, contributions from individuals and PACs reached approximately $60 million.

- As many states seek to restrict access to the ballot, New Mexico is expanding voter convenience centers and adding online and same day registration.

- Democrats increased their numbers in the state legislature in 2020, with the house now containing 45 Democrats (out of 70) and the senate 27 out of 42. The senate is no longer controlled by a coalition of Republicans and conservative Democrats. Senator Mimi Stewart, a former teacher and longtime progressive, is the Senate President Pro Tem.

- Former Senators Manny Aragon, Phil Griego, and Dianna Duran have been released from prison and have resumed their lives as private citizens.

- Drought continues to affect the Rio Grande bosque as the aging cottonwood forest declines.

~

Back home at my weekend place in the Jemez, I recently got a call from a young reporter. He was from an online publication, *New Mexico In Depth.* Luckily, the phone connection held. It often doesn't in the steep San Diego Canyon south of Jemez Springs. He was working on a story about dark money and little-known contributions from PACs to candidates in the 2020 primary. He knew I had been tracking contributions as part of a continuing effort to connect the dots between votes cast by legislators and contributions from oil and gas companies, tobacco giants, and other special interests. The research has been a continuing passion of mine, ever since the 1980s when I began to hang out at the Secretary of State's Office to look at the handwritten campaign finance reports filed there.

This time, he wanted background. I gave him a capsule history of campaign finance reform since 1997. What had taken me sixteen years inside the senate and eight more on the outside took about 20 minutes. It was just what he needed, he said.

Other reporters call about the Public Health Emergency Act, a law I helped write in 2003 that has given the Governor the authority to declare a public health emergency, quarantine the infected, close businesses, and require social distancing. "What does it allow?" they ask. "What are the limits, and what is the balance between public safety and individual rights?"

As I pressed the button on my iPhone to end the conversation with the young reporter, it occurred to me that I was back in my old role circa 1985. It felt good for the first time. I am now the communications director for Common Cause New Mexico, filling in the blanks, writing news releases, pitching stories on social media, networking, and writing reports. My files contain a boatload of information on redistricting, healthcare reform, corruption, and leadership struggles. I have become an excellent source. I always wanted to be Carl Bernstein or Bob Woodward, but now I am Deep Throat.

It has been eight years since I left the senate. Eight years filled with other elections for other people, new heroes, new villains, and new channels of communication. There were no online publications, podcasts, or Twitter feeds when I was an independent reporter. There were only three major networks, and viewers generally believed that the reports they heard were based on facts. There were lies and crooks, naturally, but the whistleblowers and reporters that ferreted them out were celebrated, not denounced as the purveyors of "fake news" or as enemies of the state.

The name-calling and verbal assaults have taken their toll. Public trust in the media has taken a nosedive. Social media has replaced *The New York Times* and documented facts are replaced by rumors, conspiracies, and repeated lies. Those that dare to question are at risk.

It is an open question whether we can keep democracy in a divided country when its guard rails have been repeatedly overrun, the rule of law undermined, science rejected, and free and open elections shamelessly challenged. What we once took for granted is no longer a given.

I don't know whether we can get those values back again.

As the weather warms and, still masked, I roam paths through the nearby bosque, I ponder these questions. Sometimes it makes me tired to think that we have to retrace our steps and dig so hard just to reach level ground. Maybe that's the point. Re-education and reinvention is the process of making a more perfect union.

And there is a strength here in the earth under my feet, and in the ebb and flow of the river. There is hope in a new democracy movement, now battle tested, composed of newer, younger groups who realize that climate change, gun violence, and continued racial and economic injustice depends on these once obscure, structural issues. They are out there knocking on doors, circulating petitions, and forging new paths toward change. This year has laid bare for them our country's deep divisions—past and present—and the difficulty of challenging the power of well financed, entrenched elites.

~

As a senator, journalist, activist, and (most of all) citizen, I have seen what Martin Luther King called "the moral arc of the universe" bending in one direction or another. I have pushed on it myself—we all have. We are watching how decisions are made, shifting our weight, and acting at critical junctures like the one we've just passed through.

We can never do enough, as I told my constituents so often. There are always ten more doors to knock on. I have tried to do my part. I have had some big successes, but often events were moved sideways or slid backward. Change moves slowly, I've learned, but I can see the results of my work—a reformed Middle Rio Grande Conservancy, the thanks a cancer survivor gives me for making her life a little easier, and the drop in teenage vehicle crashes as a result of the better training required in the Graduated Drivers License bill I carried.

My own life has had sharp dividing lines, too, but they are mere tracings compared to the bright red line drawn by COVID-19 and the culmination of four years of political upheaval. These moments in time have marked me, spun me around, set new directions, closed and opened doors. I can see this history in the rearview mirror, and it has composed the contents of this memoir—my big move from the East, my discovery of New Mexico and the community I live in, my entry into political life and the world of campaigns and elections, my election to the New Mexico Senate, my maturation as a public servant, and my departure from the senate.

I am counting on the new generations of idealists I have met along my way—members of Generations X, Y, and Z— who are uncovering inconvenient truths and fighting for equal rights or healthcare. They are veterans of Occupy Wall Street, the Parkland school shooting, and the Standing Rock and Black Lives Matter protests. They will keep on knocking on doors—thousands of them—just like I did. Some will open and some will close. Then, suddenly, there will be a clearing on the path to change.

May 2021
Albuquerque, New Mexico

About the Author

Dede Feldman was not born a progressive reformer, but her crooked path to the New Mexico Senate, through door-to-door politics, early women's campaigns, and alternative newspapers took her there. Dede grew up outside of Philadelphia and moved to Albuquerque's North Valley in 1976 where she and her husband built a pioneering solar adobe home.

She was elected to the Senate in 1996, one of the first women to represent the largely Hispanic area. During her 16 years in Santa Fe, she became a champion of healthcare and democracy reforms, environmental and consumer protection, causes she still fights for outside of the legislature.

A former teacher and journalist, she is the author of two award-winning books, *Inside the New Mexico Senate: Boots Suits and Citizens* and *Another Way Forward: Grassroots Solutions from New Mexico*. With a BA and MA from the University of Pennsylvania, Dede is currently a political commentator and non-profit consultant in Albuquerque.

Visit her at **www.dedefeldman.com**

CPSIA information can be obtained
at www.ICGtesting.com
Printed in the USA
FSHW020140280921
85018FS

9 780999 586426